Christopher and Logan
Jackson

Start ! They Score !
Shoot ! Chris Grose

Your new BBB,
Joshua Souder

www.joshuashoots.com

"Joshua Shoots! He Scores!"
The Greatest Call I Ever Made

Copyright: 2003 by Chris Madsen

Published by: JHF Publications, Incorporated
                  1700 East Garry Avenue
                  Suite 113
                  Santa Ana, California   92705

ISBN: 0-9746923-0-1

Library of Congress Cataloging-in-Publication Data applied for

First Edition: October 2003

Printed with pride by our friends at: D.M. Steele Company
                                       Fullerton, California

Cover design by: Mike Notko
idea|toaster DESIGN
Front cover photos by: Terry Notko
                       Robyn Souder
Back cover photos by: John Souder
                      Robyn Souder
Back cover copy by: JD Vercett

Inside front cover photos by: © Chris Madsen
                              Robyn Souder
Inside back cover photos by: © Chris Madsen
Inside back cover copy by: JD Vercett

Dear Reader,

At the conclusion of *"Joshua Shoots! He Scores!" The Greatest Call I Ever Made* you will find a special invitation on page 120. On behalf of everyone at JHF Publications, I'd like to thank you for your consideration.

Now, "let's get ready to lace 'em up and hit the ice!"

Sincerely,

Chris Madsen
Author

AUTHOR'S ACKNOWLEDGMENTS

We wish to thank family, friends and inspirational figures, whose names don't appear on the following pages, but nonetheless have left an indelible mark on our hearts. –The Madsens

Ken Arnold
The Bell Family
Prem Bovie-Ware
Cheryl and Victoria Calarco
The Cano Family
Rod Carew and Family
Chapman Hills Elementary Staff,
    Students and Parents (Go Pathfinders!)
The Cicero Family
Laura Dayton
Pat Dower
Paul Drake
Katie Drumm
Jim "Compe" & Lisa Duran
Christine Fisher
Dr. Chris Fotinos
Lloyd Freeberg
Galewood Community Church
Elia Garcia
Margie & Al Genovese
The Halstead Family
Karen Hartman
The "Hono" Hayes Family
Luise & Patrick Healey
The Henson Family
Dale Johnson
The Kaliski Family
Lasse Ljung
The Leith Family
The Lorenzetti Family
The Mantooth Family
The Martin Family
Debbie & Carl Mayer
Tim Mead and Family
Mighty Ducks Fans
Jennifer Mihelich
Bob & Judy Miller

Susan Miller
Matt Minery
The O'Brien Family
Jovana Ong
Jeff Proctor
PUSH America
Verne Reiniche
The Reiniche Family
The Robertson Family
The Robinson Family
Michele Ryan
The Schimpf Family
The Schmidt Family
Kathie Scott and Family
Teemu Selanne and Family
Jane Smer
The Smoter Family
James & Betsy Song
The Spargur Family
Bob & Kym Spurck
Sylvester Stallone
The Stanick Family
D.M. Steele Company
Joni Eareckson Tada
    and the staff at JAF Ministries
The Taeger Family
United Cerebral Palsy
    of The Inland Empire, CA
Jillian Vercett
The Vesio Family
Michael Villani
Eddie "Vu" Vucinic
The Wagner Family
Ken Weiser and Family
Ron Wilson and Family
Our neighbors in Hunters Glen
And all the gang at
    Ristorante Genovese in Orange, CA

"Joshua Shoots! He Scores!"
The Greatest Call I Ever Made

by

Chris Madsen

Edited by
Luise N. Healey
Lori Madsen
Kathie Scott

PUBLICATIONS
www.jhfpublications.com

This book is dedicated to two very special girls in my life: my extraordinary wife Lori, and our "dog-ter" Sugar Plum.

Lori, thank you for being *The World's Greatest Typist* and my best friend. I love you with all my heart and soul. Sugar Plum, "papa" will always cherish the days you spent patiently resting on my knee as I struggled to find the right words.

And *"Joshua Shoots! He Scores!" The Greatest Call I Ever Made* is for all the Joshua Souders of the world. May you come away inspired!

Chapter 1

From Bad Call To Best Call

I was about to receive news no one who loves their job *ever* wants to hear. What made matters worse was that the call would come from a friend.

From my hotel room at the Hyatt Printers Row in Chicago, I realized something was wrong the second I retrieved the message from my home in Orange, California. Hearing the voice of my friend say, "Hey, Chris, it's Aaron Teats calling from the Ducks," I *knew* it wasn't a call inviting me out for a round of golf or over for a family barbecue. The *last* thing Aaron had to do was give me his last name or identify his affiliation with the team. We had worked with each other for eight years, played hockey and traveled on road trips together. My wife and I had spent the previous Thanksgiving celebrating with his family and the entire Mighty Ducks Broadcasting Department.

I took a deep breath, entered my long-distance card number and called Aaron at his home. When his wife answered and said, "Oh, it's Chris," I sensed a deer-in-the-headlights sound in her voice. She handed over the phone to her husband.

Aaron got on the line, asked how I was doing, and then muttered, "You know, Chris, there's no easy way for me to say this to you, so I'm just gonna come right out and say it. We've decided we want to go in another direction. We decided that we want to change the face of Mighty Ducks television, and your services as the television play-by-play announcer for the Mighty Ducks of Anaheim are no longer needed."

My response was stunned silence. My heart had just been blown to smithereens. Within those brief sentences of a few seconds duration, my lifetime of hopes and dreams, along with nine years of loyal commitment to the Mighty Ducks of Anaheim and the community since their inception, evaporated.

I tried to gather my thoughts as best I could. I asked all the obligatory questions as to why. Aaron responded that ratings were down; they were trying to shake up the telecast; new players were being brought in; and, they thought it would be a good time to change the play-by-play voice. I was assured that it had nothing to do with my skills as a broadcaster, or me as a person. There was a new senior vice president in charge, Aaron said, and he thought it was time to initiate a change, "a change for change sake."

I never saw this coming. In fact, just that afternoon Aaron had asked my attorney, Glenn Movish, if the Ducks could have until the following Monday or Tuesday to continue discussions on a new contract.

"Aaron, is there any way I can change the call of the umpire?" I asked. My heart was in my throat.

"No."

I thanked Aaron, the Walt Disney Company, and the Mighty Ducks organization for nine memorable seasons. I told him how much I cared about him and all the wonderful people whom I had worked with over the years. As I hung up the phone, it hit me like a Scott Stevens open-ice body check. *When I return to*

Southern California, things would never be the same.

For the first time in my adult life, I was out of work. And the fact that the Ducks had waited until July 19 to render their decision left me with little chance to catch on with another hockey organization in time for the upcoming season.

That night, the uncertainty of my future left me tossing and turning. At about 2:00 a.m., my wife, Lori, snuggled up next to me and tried to assure me that "God has a plan." The warmth of her body gave me a glowing feeling of security, but by 4:30, that warmth gave way to convulsive chills.

I dreamt that I was touring Edison International Field, home of the Anaheim Angels (who were also owned by the Walt Disney Company at the time) with a group of my former co-workers. One of them snapped in my direction, "What are you doing here? You're not a part of this anymore!"

Lori looked on in horror as I sprang from the bed with uncontrollable spasms. The harder I tried to manage my involuntary twitching, the worse the panic attack became.

"That's it!" Lori cried out. "I'm calling the paramedics!"

I reached over and stopped her. "Just give me some time," I begged. "This will pass."

"Then promise me, Chris," Lori demanded, "that you're not going to let this make you sick. We'll get through this."

I had come to Chicago in July 2002 with a mission: to close one chapter of my life and to open another. My beloved father, Raymond, had passed away the summer before, and my intention was to close his estate during my stay. Walking into my dad's house, I fully expected to see him sitting at the kitchen table, reading the *Chicago Tribune*, sipping his cup of coffee (heavy cream with two sugars) and sporting his navy blue cap adorned with the U.S. flag that read, *These colors don't run!* To me, my dad was larger than life—he was the best of the best, and his passing had left an immeasurable void in my life. The feeling of not having my dad, that wonderful man to turn to with my life issues, was never more pronounced than now.

But on a brighter note, my wife's sister Annie and her husband John had welcomed their firstborn—a healthy, beautiful girl, Malia Rose Siedlinski. What an honor and privilege it was for me to be godfather to our family's new "bundle of joy."

This blessed event was overshadowed by my feelings of despair and dejection over the loss of my dream job. Each time I was forced to tell the story to relatives and friends at the christening party, it felt like a knife, cutting deeper and deeper into my soul. All the bright dreams that had come out of a lifetime commitment lay in ashes around me and left me feeling helpless and hopeless.

Three days into my new and confusing reality, I was alone in a room at my brother Marc's home on the northwest side of Chicago. Everyone in the family knew that I was in a state of shock and was giving me my space. I had barely eaten or slept since the call. As I sat there on the couch in a bewildered state, I heard a faint knock on the door.

"Come on in."

As the door swung open slowly, my twelve-year-old nephew, Nicholas, appeared and entered the room. His eyes, normally shiny and ocean blue, were bloodshot and tearing up as he sat down on the couch next to me. He looked at me and sobbed, "I just can't believe it. Mom told me you're no longer with the Ducks, and I just can't believe it."

This was one of those defining moments in life when you choose to wallow in self pity and respond, "Yes, I can't believe it either, Nicky," or you step up to the plate and try to impart one of life's lessons.

"You know, Nicky, sometimes bad things happen to good

people. For instance, how about your grandfather, our "Boompa?" He lost his right lung to cancer eighteen years ago and beat that, only to pass away from prostate cancer. Nana, your great grandmother, never smoked a day in her life, yet she died of esophageal cancer; perhaps due to all the second-hand smoke that she had inhaled over the years.

"And what about my mom, your grandmother? She developed abdominal cancer thirty-one years ago and passed on at the age of thirty-nine."

These were enormous concepts for Nicky to comprehend. He gazed off in the distance nodding his head.

"Losing my job with the Ducks is like another death in the family for me. And like any death in the family, I'm going to need time to grieve."

Nicky gathered himself, looked over at me sheepishly, and asked, "Are you going to miss it?"

"Absolutely. I'll miss everything. I'll miss the players, the travel, and, most of all, the fans. I loved what I did. I love the game."

"Who was your favorite player?"

"Well, Nicky, I guess it depends on how you define favorite. Teemu Selanne is a great player, but he also might be the nicest guy in the league. He's so full of life, and he lives life large. I just love the guy. But then you have to consider the incredible skill of Paul Kariya. Comparatively, Paul's low key, and we've always had a quiet, mutual respect for one another. But I think my favorite Duck of all time has to be Don McSween."

"Who's he?" Nicky asked as he wrinkled up his nose.

"Don was a defenseman who spent year after year down in the minors, working hard to improve his game, dreaming of the day that he'd get a shot at the big league. Then one season, a rash of injuries hit the Mighty Ducks roster hard, and Don was called up from the minors. From his very first shift in a Ducks uniform, you could tell he was poised and professional. He established himself as one of the most well conditioned athletes we've ever had. And through his tireless work ethic, he earned the respect of every one of his teammates. He finished that season by far our best defenseman. In an interview I had done with him once, he told me, 'The greatest thing about making it to the NHL is that all those nights I sat in the minors, I kept thinking to myself, *Will my son ever get the chance to see his father play in a National Hockey League game?* Just the opportunity to fulfill that dream was worth all the effort.' The following season, McSween suffered a career-ending injury in the very first game of the year in Winnipeg, but the dream he reached for was his, however, briefly."

My heart skipped a beat with that memory.

"What game will you never forget?"

I took a deep breath, and through my tightening throat, I answered, "October 8, 1993, has to rank right up there. That was the first game in franchise history, and of all the teams to play, we took on the Detroit Red Wings. We lost, but it was memorable! Five nights later, we recorded our first win against the Edmonton Oilers. And a couple of nights after that, we recorded our very first tie. Imagine an expansion team being two-two-and two through its first six games.

"And Nicky, I'll never forget the very first playoff game at home against Phoenix. The Pond was filled with a sea of white *Fowl Towels* waving in the air. When the red light went on and I got my cue to go on the air, I felt the goose bumps on my arms and the hair on the back of my neck stand straight up. It's what Stanley Cup playoff hockey is all about!"

And then, Nicky asked me *THE* question: "Uncle Chris, what's the best call you ever made?"

I swallowed hard in an effort to maintain my composure, and then I continued.

"The best call I ever made? Well, I called the first goal in franchise history scored by Sean Hill. I called the first win in franchise history against Edmonton. I'll always remember goaltender Ron Tugnutt skating off the ice, shaking his victorious fist in the air, and head coach Ron Wilson jumping up and down behind the bench. That was a great moment. I remember the time that Roman Oksiuta set up Paul Kariya for his fiftieth goal, which was the first time 'P.K.' reached that benchmark in his young career.

"But you know what Nicky?" I continued. "Let me think about that for a while. I'll come up with an answer."

"Do you want to go outside and play some catch?" Nicky asked.

"Uncle Chris really doesn't feel like doing much of anything right now. I've got some thinking to do. So why don't you give me the room for a while, and maybe a bit later on, I'll put on a glove and we'll toss the ball around. Okay?"

"Okay," he agreed as he hugged me and left the room.

So there I was, sitting in the den that I had sat in so many times before with my father from whom I often sought advice and guidance. God knows how much I wished he were here. If only I could rest my troubled head on his reassuring shoulder. If only I could wrap my arms around Dad's steady frame. If only I could whisper my heartfelt concerns into his attentive ear, and then listen as he responded with his unique sense of great direction and wisdom.

But truthfully, Nicky's question was one that only *I* could answer. "What's the best call you ever made?" kept ringing in my head. Honestly, my energy level was so sapped that all I wanted to do was curl up in a ball and die. My life felt like it was over.

Like a migraine, Nicky's question took over and blinded me from everything else except searching out the answer.

All of a sudden, like a high stick to the side of the head to the guy with the identity crisis, the guy who could only see himself as the television play-by-play announcer of the Mighty Ducks of Anaheim, I saw the answer with absolute clarity. *The greatest call I ever made happened through a chance meeting with a little boy who would change my life forever.*

Chapter 2

Chance Meeting

As the television play-by-play voice of the franchise, my job was to "call them as I see them." The way I saw it, the Mighty Ducks 1993-1994 inaugural season was a honeymoon, and the love affair with the fans was in full bloom. Everything the marketing and public relations departments came up with turned to gold. Their formula was simple: *Build a Mighty Ducks adventure, and the fans will come.*

That's exactly what the front office did in February of 1994. They hosted the first ever "FanFair," creating a three-level, carnival-like experience inside the Arrowhead Pond. The main concourse and club level were converted into games of chance, along with some autograph booths where fans waited in line, eager to take pictures with their favorite players.

The real action was down at ice level where insulation had been placed over the gigantic frozen sheet. Fans got a charge out of walking on what was normally the playing surface. At center ice stood the Mystery Box game where, for a monetary donation, fans chose a gift box and won a hidden item. The prizes ranged from an unpretentious Mighty Ducks T-shirt to a coveted Mighty Ducks team autographed jersey. Off to the side was the "How Hard Can You Shoot the Puck?" booth and a dunk tank for the coaches. If you had an accurate arm, this was the place to be. FanFair was a feast for the fans with something for everyone.

One of my duties that afternoon was to conduct the first-ever Mighty Ducks Memorabilia Auction.

"The last item up for bid," I barked, "is a beautifully framed, authentic Mighty Ducks team jersey signed by every player and coach on this year's squad. What a stunning conversation piece this would make in any office or family room!

"Can I get an opening bid of $400? I have 400, looking for five. Five hundred, looking for six." The key was to pit one member of the audience against another. Like lightning, the numbers skyrocketed.

"I have 900, looking for 1,000. I have a bid of $1,200 in the front row. Twelve hundred dollars, going once; a bid of $1,200 going twice; $1,200 a third and final time. Sold for $1,200!

"Congratulations, and thank you for your generosity."

What an adrenaline rush! I had to take a walk just to simmer down. I put down the microphone and joined my wife. Taking her by the arm, we made our way through the Zamboni entrance, which was packed with people. Off in the distance I heard a child's voice cry out, "Chris! Hey, Chris!"

Though I heard the voice, I couldn't see where it was coming from. As the bodies parted in front of us, a petite woman with long brown hair approached. She looked me straight in the eye and said, "Mr. Madsen, that voice you hear is my son, and he is one of your biggest fans. Would you mind coming over to talk to him?"

Flabbergasted that I had a "fan," I replied, "Absolutely. You know, I can hear him, but I can't see him. Where is he?"

"Come, follow me," she said.

Lori and I followed her, and then I saw him. There, peeking out from behind the passing crowd, was a wheelchair-bound little boy with a wealth of curly blond hair tucked under a Mighty Ducks cap. His large brown eyes were made even larger by a pair of oversized glasses. Sporting a Mighty Ducks sweatshirt, he frantically waved his left hand still trying to garner my attention. His thin right arm bent upward, and his hand contorted inward against his chest. The entire length of his legs was set in steel braces, and his feet fell limp on the chair's footrests.

Before I could utter a single syllable, he called out, "Chris, I watch you all the time."

I knelt down and gazed into the sparkling eyes of my newfound fan. This was the first time in the five months I had been with the team that someone actually approached me.

"You even know what my name is?" I asked curiously.

"Oh, Joshua never misses a game if it's on TV. By the way, my name is Robyn. I'm Joshua's mother. And this is Joshua's sister, Sarah, and Josh's friend, Joshua Millsap."

"My pleasure to meet you," I said, nodding to them. "I'm Chris Madsen, and this is my wife, Lori. So, Joshua, what's your last name?"

"Souder. S-O-U-D-E-R," he answered as his dark eyes beamed with delight.

"How old are you, Josh?"

"Nine."

"Well, nine-year-old Joshua Souder, your mom says you never miss a game."

"Ever since the inaugural game, I was hooked!" Joshua exclaimed. The boy's smile was contagious. "And you, sir, are the best."

"Somebody get this boy a jersey!" I fired back. Looking closely at Josh's cap, I noted, "Joshua, it looks like you've commandeered a couple of autographs."

Robyn stepped in. "You know, when I bought the tickets to FanFair, I thought that everything was included. Silly me," she said placing her right hand on her chest. Her face flushed with embarrassment. "This is a charitable fundraiser. I should have known better."

"No problem. We'll get Josh plenty of autographs."

"Well, the wife of one of your players, Pam Williams, was so nice that she took us to see her husband, David, and your mascot, Wild Wing, and they were kind enough to autograph Joshua's cap."

"So, Joshua," I teased, "you think you know your Mighty Ducks hockey, huh?"

"Yep," he answered confidently. His clear brown eyes never wavered.

"So, what number does David Williams wear?" I asked.

"Number 4," he shouted back.

"You are correct, sir. High-five me!" I said as his tiny left hand connected with my left hand. "Who's our starting goaltender?"

"Number 31, Guy Hebert."

As we high-fived again, a crowd formed around us, and I pushed up the volume.

"Who is Guy's backup in goal?"

"Number 35, Mikhail Shtalenkov."

"High-five me," I commanded. This time, it was met with a generous round of applause. I had another question for Joshua, though. "Who's our team captain, and what's his number?"

"Number 24, Troy Loney."

This time our post-correct answer celebration was met with thunderous applause. I glanced over at Lori. She was dabbing away a tear from her eye, and as Joshua and I embraced, I declared, "Ladies and gentlemen, I would like to introduce you to Joshua Souder, my Broadcasting Booth Buddy."

The ovation rang throughout the lower bowl of the arena, and that's when I informed my brand new friend, "Always leave them wanting more." I barked to the crowd, "Joshua and I will be appearing tonight at the Long Beach Holiday Inn at 8 and 11 o'clock. We recommend the veal. Be sure to tip your waiter or waitress!"

After a mixture of laughs and groans, the crowd began to disperse, and I turned to Robyn and asked, "Have you been out to a game?"

"Heavens, no," she confessed as she shook her head. "We came to FanFair because the tickets were only ten dollars. We couldn't possibly afford to come to a real game."

"Well, you won't have to worry about tickets anymore," I assured her.

"Chris," Joshua interrupted, "would you sign my autograph book?"

"Well, Josh," I said, "you now hold the dubious distinction of being the first person to ask me for my autograph as the television voice of the Mighty Ducks of Anaheim. How about that?"

"Sounds good to me," Josh replied as he handed over a white 4" x 6" vinyl autograph book.

With black Sharpie in hand, I wrote as I called out, "*Joshua shoots! He scores! Ducks win! All my love, Chris Madsen.*"

Joshua rocked back and forth in his wheelchair with delight and extended his left hand for another high-five. As I held Joshua's hand, I turned to Robyn and said, "Come on. Follow me. I'll get you my card. We'll exchange numbers. Don't worry, we'll definitely get you and Joshua out to see a game this season."

As we walked toward my office, Joshua deftly maneuvered his electric wheelchair by a control knob positioned beneath his left hand.

"So, Joshua, I'm curious," I said. "Of all the coaches and players at FanFair today, why did you want to see me?"

"Because I want to be a sports announcer, just like you," explained Joshua.

I stepped in front of the wheelchair. Joshua applied the brakes quickly. As I squatted down in front of him and placed my right hand on his left shoulder, I assured him, "Joshua, from what I saw today, I think you'll make a magnificent announcer!" Joshua's big grin beamed like a jack-o-lantern on Halloween night. Placing my business card in his left hand, I reminded him, "Always remember, your Broadcasting Booth Buddy is just a phone call away."

"Thanks, Chris," Josh said appreciatively. "You're the best!"
I turned to Lori and put my arm around her, then with great pride I boasted, "Did you hear what Josh said?"

"What's that, honey?" Lori questioned.

"Josh said, 'I'm the best!'" I announced, my head at this point barely fitting through the width of the hallway.

Lori chuckled as Josh interrupted, "It's true! You, sir, are the best!"

Little did I know that this meeting with Joshua Souder was not by chance, but was rather a significant step in God's plan for our lives-Joshua's and mine.

Chapter 3

Stepping Stones

No matter what the field of endeavor, if you want to be the best, you must study the best. Prior to the age of twelve, as much as I enjoyed impersonating Chicago's local broadcasters, I aspired to be a doctor. I admired the father of my classmate, Bobby Burdick. Bobby's dad was my mother's physician, and I saw first-hand how much he really cared for his patients. His compassionate bedside manner had always left a positive impression on me. I was certain that I, too, wanted to help other people just like Dr. Burdick did. That was until I saw how difficult it was to give a family devastating news. Dr. Burdick delivered the bad news to my family in the spring of 1971 when he informed us that there really was no hope for my mother—it was only a matter of time before she would be leaving us.

Mom's cancer had spread aggressively to her liver and pancreas. Her once healthy skin color had changed to a sickly yellowish hue. As young as I was, I sensed how this awful transformation and the loss of much of her hair made my mother feel very self-conscious about her appearance and understandably so.

Being underage for hospital visitation rights, I was shielded from the agonizing treatments my mother had to endure. My older sister, Karen, once told me that a series of cobalt treatments left Mom so radioactive that the hospital staff had actually cordoned off an area around her bed so no one could get any closer.

Late in her condition, Dad snuck me in for a visit on Mother's Day, 1971. I carefully carried a card I had made for Mom out of construction paper that featured her on the cover with long brown hair, sparkling brown eyes, holding her purse in one hand and pushing a shopping cart with the other.

As Dad and I stepped into the shared hospital room, the pungent smell of rubbing alcohol permeated my very being. The first bed was empty. Walking past the shear curtain, I found Mom. With the head of the bed raised, she was propped from the waist up. Wearing a pale pink terrycloth robe, Mom's beaming face was beautiful. She looked every bit an angel to me.

"Christopher, come give your mommy a big kiss," she requested as I climbed carefully onto the bed with her and laid my head on her chest. I remember vividly how wonderful it felt and how delighted I was to be so close to her again. I presented her with my homemade Mother's Day card. She exclaimed, "This reminds Mommy of our walks together to the A&P!"

"When are you coming home, Mom?" I asked.

"Not for a while, honey," she responded, her voice cracking in mid-sentence. "Have you been listening to Dad and Nana?"

Overcome by her previous answer, I just nodded "yes," and I tried to cuddle up closer.

Mom continued, "Nana says you haven't been singing as much. Why don't you put on an Andy Williams's album today and sing *Hello Dolly* as a Mother's Day gift for her when you get home? Okay?"

"Okay," I whispered.

"Now give your mommy a big hug and a kiss before you go."

"I don't want to go!"

"Mommy doesn't want you to go either," she said as her brown eyes filled with tears.

"I love you, Mommy," I said, gripping her hand.

"I love you, too."

"Good night. God bless you, Mom."

"Good night. God bless you, Christopher Michael."

When it was time to separate, my dad and grandmother literally had to peel me away from my ailing mother. During a very quiet ride home from West Suburban Hospital in Oak Park, the tears rolled down my cheeks and chin as I instinctively realized I might never see my mother alive again.

Three days later, Mom passed over to a better place.

On the morning of my mother's funeral, after friends and relatives had passed by to pay their last respects, Dad took my sister, Karen, and me by the hand, and along with my brother, Marc, we solemnly approached the casket. With each step, I felt the building of an emotional tidal wave. Behind us, I heard sniffling and sobbing. Gazing over into the casket in disbelief, each one of us, like dominoes, one by one, turned and buried our faces in our father's chest. Silently I cried out in protest of this most sacred loss—the separation of mother and child. Internalizing the gut-wrenching pain, I was resolute in my conviction to be strong for my father.

Dad embraced us and kissed the tops of our heads. As I looked up from his white dress shirt, I saw my dad's chin quiver and his eyes well up with tears. Marc, Karen and I were escorted to our seats as Dad approached Mom one last time. He gently reached in, placed his hand on hers, whispered his final goodbye and leaned forward to kiss her on her forehead.

Dad looked over at the morticians and nodded. Two gentlemen dressed in black suits, white shirts, black ties and white formal gloves tucked the white casket linens around Mom's head and torso. Then slowly they guided the lid downward. This surreal scene seemed to play out in slow motion. Gently they sealed the chamber, but to my ears it was as though I heard a thick, cold steel door slam shut. My head snapped back, numbed by the revelation that I would never again see my mom on this earth.

The passing of my mom, Cecelia Florence Madsen, was painful to say the least. Pain and sorrow engulfed a surviving mother, a husband, two sons, a daughter, a sister, a brother, a sister-in-law, a brother-in-law, nieces, nephews, friends, teachers, and co-workers.

Mom's death delivered two eye-opening lessons: how one precious life, however brief, can touch so many others; and, how some visits to the doctor don't have a happy ending.

I felt so cheated then, losing my mother so early in my life, and I still do to this day. At the age of twelve, I was the youngest of her three children, and she had been ill for almost half of my life. During the brief time we had together, though, we were like best friends. I will always cherish our walks to the park, the grocery store, and on those special occasions when I'd meet my mom at her office and walk home with her. As we strolled along, I'd share what happened in my day; she'd share what happened in hers. We'd talk about what the evening had in store for us. We were close, as every mother and son would hope to be.

The highlight of my memories of my mother was how secure I felt just holding her hand as we crossed the street. She grasped my hand tight enough to assure me how much she'd protect me, yet gentle enough to convey the notion that some steps must be taken on my own.

The loss of a parent, especially at such a young age, accelerates the maturation process. I observed more and listened better, especially to my instincts. Listening to that inner voice, I realized I couldn't become the bearer of bad news; couldn't reconcile the agony that accompanies it. Listening to my heart, I took a conscience step forward in the direction of one of my true passions—sports. My childhood ambition of becoming a doctor was no longer an option; becoming a professional play-by-play man was my new goal.

Whether it was watching games on television, or tuning in on the radio, or even using my nana's Zenith stereo late at night, I was mentally transported into some faraway game, dreaming of the day when I, too, would be sitting behind a microphone "calling the action." I remember sitting in my bedroom on summer nights in Chicago, fine tuning the stereo to listen to Marty Brenneman and Joe Nuxall on WLW in Cincinnati as they called the action of my favorite baseball team, the Cincinnati Reds. As the distant radio waves faded in and out, I feverishly played with the control knob to tune the game back in. My efforts were rewarded when Brenneman declared, "And this one belongs to the Reds!"

But no one influenced me more than the local Chicago broadcasters. Legendary hall-of-famer Jack Brickhouse, the long-time voice of the Chicago Cubs, provided a familiar soundtrack on WGN TV. I'll never forget his call as future hall-of-famer Billy Williams leveled the bat over the plate. "Here's the windup and the pitch. Swung on. Deep fly ball to right field, back she goes, back, back, back. Hey-hey! That a boy, Billy! Cubs in the lead! Wee!"

Chicago Bulls play-by-play man Jim Durham, in my opinion, was one of the finest basketball announcers ever. He had this very distinct call—crisp and clear and extremely descriptive.

Then, of course, Chicago had Harry Caray, first on the south side with the White Sox and then on the north side with the Cubs. Now there's a guy who got it right. He lived large and broadcasted games even bigger. "It might be, it could be, it is!" was Harry's signature home run call. What I loved about Harry was that he seemed like a "regular Joe," a guy who'd sit next to you at the corner bar and shoot the breeze. But this regular Joe just so happened to have a microphone in front of him, along with a national television audience, and got paid to call baseball. Most importantly, he never forgot the fans, and that was the secret to his success.

But to me, at the top of the broadcasting echelon, nobody came close to longtime play-by-play announcer Lloyd Pettit, the voice of the Chicago Blackhawks. Pettit had this deep bass-y voice that somehow captured every nook and cranny of the excitement of National Hockey League action. In the background, I'd hear the roar of the crowd start off very calmly and then build to the Blackhawks' blue line, build even more to the red line, build even greater as the puck crossed the opposing team's blue line into the offensive zone. Then I'd hear "Aahh" if they came close to the net, and if they missed, I'd hear "Oohh." Throughout the puck's journey, Pettit was on top of the action. He was magnificent, and he *was* my broadcasting idol.

Sunday night home games broadcast from the old Chicago Stadium at 1800 West Madison Street were a ritual during hockey season. I'd sit on the living room couch clutching my transistor radio with my eyes closed, envisioning every play while listening to Blackhawks games through an earpiece. Meanwhile, Nana sat knitting on the other end of the couch. I'll never forget one game in particular against the Boston Bruins. The

Blackhawks and the B's were tied late in the game. "Jimmy Pappin with a wrist shot and a goal!" rang through the earpiece. I jumped up and screamed, "He scored! He scored! The Blackhawks win it!" I heard the crowd go out of its mind—and so did I! My poor grandmother was scared half to death thinking I just had some sort of attack. But that's the knack Pettit had—he had the ability to draw in the listener.

When I was a kid, getting a ticket to a Blackhawks game was virtually impossible. Every night the attendance at the old Chicago Stadium was listed as 16,666 when we all knew, as probably did the Fire Marshall, that the crowd was a much higher number than that. They packed them in like sardines—the fans loved their Blackhawks hockey.

As a child growing up in Chicago during the 1960s, following the Blackhawks became my passion. Whether through home games on the radio or a steady dose of road games on WGN-TV, I was mesmerized by the awesome power and grace of the "Golden Jet" Bobby Hull, the slippery stick handling skills of Stan Mikita, and the gutsy determination of goaltender Glenn Hall. Imagine facing one hundred mile an hour slap shots without the aid of a mask!

But game after game, year after year, as the players came and went, there remained one constant—the soundtrack of Chicago Blackhawks hockey was Lloyd Pettit. Pettit called the game the way hockey has to be called: with passion, precision and instinct. Many times an athlete is referred to as a "student of the game," meaning that he or she studies a particular athlete or team, dissects footage, or becomes fluent in the history of the game. By the time I was nine years old, much like an athlete, I had become a student of Lloyd Pettit. My "education" took a quantum leap forward on Christmas Day, 1967.

Chapter 4

A Life-Changing Present

It was a Madsen family tradition for all my aunts, uncles, and cousins to gather at our home on Chicago's northwest side for a festive Christmas celebration. On this particular occasion, circa 1967, a rectangular box from my Auntie Dianne and Uncle Mike about three inches deep, a foot-and-a-half wide, and three feet long, meticulously wrapped in red and green holiday paper, rested underneath the Christmas tree. The mere size of this colossal present caught my attention.

I was thrilled, of course, when I discovered that the "To" tag was addressed to my brother, Marc, and me! I couldn't wait to open it! After what seemed like an eternity for our turn to open a gift, Marc and I tore into the paper. There in big, bold print was **Bobby Hull Hockey**! Eureka! We had struck gold!

I was floored by the great opportunities that awaited me: challenging my family and friends to tabletop hockey games! I was absolutely enamored with this present, primarily because I'd be able to apply names to the players and "call" the movement of the puck. This was a dream come true!

My brother Marc and I went at it every evening. Although the game was called Bobby Hull Hockey, surprisingly, there weren't any Blackhawk players in the set. In the box were caricatures of Montreal Canadiens and Toronto Maple Leaf players. But Marc and I, being loyal Blackhawk fans, taped emblems over some of the players' sweaters and made believe they were the likes of Chico Maki, Stan Mikita, Bobby Hull, Giles Marrotte, Doug Jarrett, and Glen Hall "between the pipes."

Night after night, our makeshift Blackhawks took to the ice with their crests taped over the uniforms of the Maple Leafs. They squared off against the likes of Montreal's Jean Beliveau, J. C. Trembley, Serge Savard, Yvon Cournoyer, and Henri Richard. In the Montreal glitter and glamour, the Blackhawks and the Canadiens went toe to toe, complete with a cappella renditions of the U.S. and Canadian national anthems, of course. Once the puck was dropped, the action was fast and furious. "Beliveau shoots! Big save, Hall!"

I admit I got my butt royally kicked by my brother, Marc. Pretty consistently, too, if the truth be told. It wasn't that I couldn't play well—when I challenged my other friends to a game, I'd usually dominate. But when I played against my brother, I was more interested in calling the action while trying to keep up with the pace of the game. "Bobby Hull with a slap shot and a goal!" My only concern was following the puck and identifying players rather than actually putting the puck in the net. That's how I began to hone my announcing skills. This much beloved and often used Christmas present was the impetus for my broadcasting career. My won-loss record, however, left much to be desired.

Chapter 5

Furthering My Education

By the time I reached high school, between my vivid imagination and the way I had developed a knack for announcing all types of sports, be it baseball, basketball, or hockey, many of my friends would entice me to "call" games.

I'll never forget being involved in a very raucous intramural basketball game in the gymnasium at my high school, Luther North, on Chicago's northwest side. All of a sudden, I broke into my "Jim Durham impersonation" and assigned Chicago Bulls players' names to every classmate on the floor. Of course, the big guy in the middle was Artis Gilmore. I was Norm Van Leer, the guy running the plays. Typically, the guys out on the wings were Chet Walker or Bob Love.

As luck would have it, I had become so skillful at this that people actually demanded that I "call" their games. I was even asked to call the play-by-play action on the public address system for some of Luther North High School basketball games. I thought the players, coaches, and officials would find it terribly distracting, but nobody seemed to mind. All the while, my broadcasting skills were being perfected.

During my senior year of high school in 1976, I developed a cyst at the base of my spine, which required surgery. The timing couldn't have been worse. I had just come off a Private School League "honorable mention" baseball season in 1975. I was considered one of the top catchers in the state and had been contacted by as many as thirteen major league ball clubs at the time. However, after the operation, it was evident that I really couldn't catch any more my senior year. Soon after surgery, I realized the healing process was going to take far more time than the eight weeks the doctors had first projected.

Over the course of the next year and a half, I ate the majority of my meals standing up. I watched the majority of my television lying down. I wasn't able to drive a car because I could only lean to one side or the other, which made it extremely uncomfortable. My closest friends, Mark Schaeffer and Jay Dower, carted me about town.

I started my freshman year at Triton College in River Grove, Illinois, and then in 1978 headed west to Scottsdale Community College in Arizona to play the fall season of baseball and take in my prerequisites. In the spring of 1979, I returned to Chicago for another semester at Wright Junior College. All the while, I was a Dean's List student. All the while, I dreamed about playing baseball at the same level that I was able to play before. And all the while, my goal was to get a college scholarship.

My father had spent quite a bit of money on my education considering that through the years 1972 to 1976, my tuition at Luther North High School ran between $800 and $1200 per year. These numbers may seem like a bargain nowadays, but thirty years ago, trust me, that was a lot of money. I told Dad that if I went to college, I was going to foot the bill and that he would not be responsible for any of it, not even a penny. As a result, I worked *extremely* hard in the classroom and on the baseball diamond.

And it paid off. I was named "Rookie of the Year" of my Wright Jr. College baseball team and was eventually offered a scholarship to Lewis University in Romeoville, Illinois. Lewis, a relatively small Catholic college, is located about 45 minutes southwest of Chicago. Its Flyers NAIA Conference baseball program had drawn rave reviews having won national championships in 1974, 1975, and 1976. I was somewhat familiar with Lewis because my sister, Karen, attended the university in 1972. Now it was my turn. I attended this fine institution on a partial baseball scholarship; the remainder of the tuition I secured through a bank college loan.

As an aspiring broadcaster, what intrigued me most about Lewis was their campus radio station 88.7 FM, WLRA. They were in need of a part-time sports anchor and men's basketball analyst. I auditioned for both and was granted the positions. Imagine, a radio gig, a baseball scholarship, and a quality education. Talk about hitting a trifecta!

Chapter 6

Bad Luck, Good Luck

y junior year at Lewis University was a unique one. Even though I was a junior *academically*, I was considered a sophomore *athletically*, because I had to sit out a year due to my back injury.

The Lewis University Flyers had an absolutely stacked varsity baseball team. As we went through the roster, I noticed more and more that I was being tabbed as a "utility" player, although I had just about never missed a game on the varsity squad since my sophomore year in high school. Things were going to be far different at this level. So I accepted the frosh-soph team assignment.

We had a cast of characters—what a wonderful group of guys they were. Our coach, Bob Hartman, pulled me aside and told me that I was going to be one of his leaders. I was at least a year older than most of the other guys, and he expected me to help mold this club with him.

I roamed from the outfield to third base but, once again, found a home at my natural position as a catcher. By the time we had made it to the final weeks of both the frosh-soph and varsity season, they decided to bring me up and give me some time on the varsity level. I didn't see much action though—there were two terrific catchers, Ty Clover, the starter, and Greg Leoni, our backup, in front of me. Whenever I had the opportunity, I rose to the occasion.

Our team was going to the College World Series in Nashville to represent the NAIA, the National Athletic Intercollegiate Association. The coaches were forced to make a difficult decision. Would I earn a spot on the roster or would Brian Jendra, another frosh-soph player? Brian had a fabulous year, but was it good enough to earn that coveted spot?

Unfortunately for me, I developed a hand injury late in the season. While diving for a foul ball, I fell down some dugout steps and wrenched my left thumb backwards. What made matters worse was that it was my catching hand and the bottom hand of my grip at the plate. They put it in a partial cast, from which it had yet to fully recover. So the coaches' decision was relatively easy—Brian was healthy, Brian was good and Brian was getting that final spot on the roster.

Meanwhile, WJOL-FM, an ABC affiliate in Joliet, decided that since a local team made it to the College World Series, they would give the broadcasters of the club, John Mason and Joe Dejanovich, the opportunity to broadcast the games over local ABC radio. When the station realized that I wasn't on the active roster, they asked if I'd be willing to step in and do some analysis of the game. Since I couldn't suit up to play, I thought I might as well do the next best thing and said, "Count me in!" Off to Nashville we went.

Fortunately for me, Lewis had a great run and went all the way to the College World Series championship game against Grand Canyon College. I had the opportunity to work with John and Joe on as many as five games.

When you're sitting in the broadcast booth with your headset on, completely "in the zone" and into the game, it's easy to lose yourself in the action. On the bus ride back to the hotel after the game, I replayed in my mind significant moments and analyzed how I described the sequence and took notes on what I might say and do differently if the situation should present itself again.

Following every broadcast I'd call Dad and Nana, who had tuned in back home in Chicago, to get their feedback. Dad took notes during the game and passed along well-intentioned pointers like, "Let your emotions come through the radio" or "E-nun-ci-ate your words cor-rect-ly."

"Oh, Raymond," Nana chimed in. "Chris, honey, I thought you were great!"

"Thanks Nana! But Dad's got a point."

Dad's closing line was, "This is a big opportunity for you, Son. Prepare even harder for the next game because you never know who is listening."

Chapter 7

Anybody Listening?

JD Vercett is an alumnus of Lewis University who I got to know quite well during my junior year there. He and his friends would drive out to Lewis to take in the occasional Flyer baseball game. But I got to know JD best when he filled in as a substitute teacher for Jim Boles, who was our usual sports broadcasting teacher. JD had built a solid reputation on Lewis's campus for the four years of excellent work at WLRA, the campus' radio station. JD took a keen interest in what I had to offer. He worked with me in polishing my on-air skills and at becoming a better writer. Perhaps it was JD Vercett who really set my path off in the right direction when it came to sports broadcasting.

They say timing is everything. JD was visiting his mother in nearby Lockport, Illinois, while I was broadcasting those NAIA playoff games on WJOL. He tuned in, liked what he heard, and left a note on my dorm room door to call him when the College World Series was over. Immediately upon my return from Nashville, I responded.

JD had carved himself quite a niche as the daytime voice of Sports Phone, a telephone service provided by a company called Phone Programs of Illinois, Inc., that had garnered a loyal, mass audience with scores, interviews, and highlights provided 24 hours a day. He suggested that I consider coming to work for Sports Phone. He also recommended that I put together an audition tape. When he asked if I had ever dialed in to Sports Phone, I responded, "Of course." I lied. Overcome by a moment of truth, I confided to JD that I felt I needed a bit more seasoning when it came to sports reporting, and when, in my opinion, I progressed to a higher level on the air, I'd take him up on his offer.

One Monday night while working in the campus radio station at WLRA, I got on the phone and called Sports Phone. There on the end of the line was announcer David Schuster. He ran down a list of NBA and NHL scores, had a news item on Muhammad Ali and closed out with the day's transactions in Major League baseball. It seemed like a lot of information, but, as I checked my stopwatch, it was all tucked inside of 60 seconds. I decided to write my own script and send in my own tape. Within a few days, I received a response.

The following week I was invited to interview for a position. After my classes, I drove downtown to the John Hancock Building and took the elevator to Suite 3101. There to greet me was JD Vercett. He introduced me to all the announcers at Sports Phone: Schuster, Bill Ezrin, Jerry Erlich, Fred Huebner, and Bill Korbel. He then introduced me to the company's general manager, Walter Burch, who conducted the interview. It started at three, and 15 minutes into the process he asked how I'd feel about going into the booth to produce a sports report for him. I said, "No problem." I had mine all ready. I went in with my audio tapes in hand, popped them into the tape decks, set the microphone level, and off I went. I had 59 and 9/10ths seconds to do it. I hit it in 59 flat. Burch said, "You're hired!"

I sat alongside the voices that would become so familiar to me over the next few years. David Schuster used me as a writer that evening. As news came across the wire, I'd turn them into short stories that he would use as filler between scores and highlights. As the evening wore on, Schuster told me that when I felt comfortable, I could go in and knock out a report or two. I did. And with each report, I gained more confidence.

That night driving down the Stevenson Expressway to Lewis University, I had to make a tough decision. Should I forego my baseball scholarship and dedicate my time to my schoolwork and my newfound job? Or could I convince the "powers that be" at Lewis to allow me to retain my baseball scholarship, sacrifice the spring season, and use me as an opportunity to promote their sports broadcasting program? Besides, the campus radio station had been "dark" for months. The transmitter was in disrepair, and the school didn't have a replacement in the budget any time soon.

The next afternoon I sat down with Athletic Director Paul Ruddy and Head Baseball Coach Irish O'Reilly, and they enthusiastically agreed that it would be in everyone's best interests that my scholarship remain in tact and that I continue my education. They also agreed that I should accept the position with Sports Phone and would design a curriculum around that—a curriculum that would allow me to graduate on time in June of 1981, which I did with honors.

Graduating from Lewis meant so much to me, but I think it mattered even more so to my father. I became the first Madsen to ever earn a college degree. As soon as I had my diploma in hand, I hit the ground running.

Chapter 8

Chance Of A Lifetime

In a span of four years, I made the ascent from part-time employee to office general manager of Phone Programs of Illinois. I learned all facets of the telephone programming industry, which later proved to be invaluable. All the while I networked.

I had made my way into the radio broadcast booth for the University of Illinois-Chicago Flames hockey team of the Central Collegiate Hockey Association. I worked as an analyst alongside Chicago sportscaster Les Grobstein on weekend home games and made the transition to television play-by-play announcer when the Flames games aired on SportsChannel-Chicago TV. I also became friends with Tom Greene, a local Chicago radio broadcaster whom I admired because of his laid-back delivery. Tom gave me the opportunity to fill in for him at WCLR-FM in Skokie/Chicago on those mornings when he was on vacation.

In 1984, the Chicago Cubs ended 39 years of frustration

when the team won the National League East title. This put the "toddle" back in Chicago, that toddling town, and set in motion another series of life-changing events.

JD Vercett, who had moved up to assistant general manager at Phone Programs, made arrangements with Kobelt Travel Service, the official travel agency of the Cubs, to conduct a contest, which offered three lucky fans an all-expense paid trip to San Diego to watch the Cubs take on the Padres in the National League Championship Series.

An ad ran in the *Chicago Sun-Times* and on Sports Phone that instructed fans on how to enter the contest. With only three days lead time to promote the giveaway, more than 10,000 entries came pouring into our offices. There was a glitch, however. The promotions department expected six *pairs* of tickets from the travel agency, but instead only three pairs of tickets or just six *individual* trips were provided. This created a dilemma—we had to travel a reporter, a chaperone (which happened to be me), and the assistant general manager. Corporate made the decision that since the ads mentioned three trips to see the Cubs in San Diego, we would give away three *single* trips to Southern California.

Three names were selected. We would meet our guests two days later at Chicago's O'Hare International Airport. As I awaited their arrival, I struck up a conversation with friend and long-time Cubs public address announcer, Wayne Messmer.

No sooner had we started chatting when a beautiful girl with pretty brown hair and soulful brown eyes entered the terminal. I motioned to Wayne and said, "Now why can't one of my winners look like that?" Suddenly, a travel agent from Kobelt intercepted this beauty. They hooked a U-turn and started walking in my direction. "Chris, I'd like to introduce you to one of your winners. This is Lori."

Hot dog! I remember thinking.

Over the next four days, Lori and I, along with many of the fans on the Cubs charter, dined, danced and discovered San Diego, and looked on helplessly as the Cubs dropped three straight games to the Padres.

It came to an all-too-soon end.

Boarding the fan charter plane to return to Chicago, I noticed Lori sitting seven rows behind me. We exchanged a cordial wave to each other as I took my window seat in the eleventh row.

The flight attendants made their way down the aisle encouraging all passengers to stow away all their personal belongings and to fasten their seatbelts. The captain gave a brief overview of our flight plan from San Diego to Chicago and concluded with, "Flight attendants, prepare for take off."

Accompanied by a violent vibration from the tail of the cabin that reverberated throughout the fuselage, the plane surged forward as we began to taxi down the runway.

Must be a heavy load, I thought to myself.

The plane seemed to strain to gain the necessary speed for liftoff. No sooner had the nose of the plane left the ground, the pilot dropped it back down and slammed on the brakes. Everyone lunged forward. The craft groaned as someone shouted out, "Somebody drag a foot!" That comment drew some uneasy laughs. Screeching to a halt, our bodies were thrown back into our seats.

Now for those of us who hadn't spent the seventh-inning stretch in the beer line, this was a heart-in-your-throat moment if there ever was one!

Adrenaline surged throughout my body as I felt my pulse drumming in my ears. I grabbed the arm of the gentleman next to me whose face was as red as a furnace and asked, "Are you alright?"

"My wife and I are a bit shaken as you can imagine, but we'll be okay."

The captain announced, "Ladies and gentlemen, this is your captain speaking. We have an oil pressure problem in one of the engines. We apologize for the short stop. Please remain in your seats until we return to the terminal."

I knelt on my seat and turned back to locate Lori and found her sitting with her head in her hands. I slumped back down in my chair and thanked God for protecting us.

For the next 45 minutes we sat out on the tarmac, without air conditioning. As they towed the aircraft back to the gate, the crew told us to expect significant delays as a replacement part was being flown in from Los Angeles—something every weary traveler wants to hear! In other words, once they *think* they've got this thing fixed, they're going to put us back on the same plane. Yikes!

Once inside the terminal, I spotted a shaken Lori who confessed, "That was scary! I've said my *Act of Contrition* so many times, I lost count!"

"Look, why don't you call your family and tell them about the delay. Then I'll take you for a bite to eat."

Three hours later, we boarded the same plane. But this time as I took my seat, Lori plopped down in the seat next to me. I looked at her. She looked at me. We sat in uneasy silence for a few moments.

"How are you doing?" she asked.

"Well, when I get nervous, I get a little quiet," I replied. "And right now, I'm pretty nervous."

More silence. Lori broke the ice.

"Well, there's only one thing I'd regret if this plane does go down, Chris."

"What's that?"

"Not having kissed you the way I wanted to!" And with that, she grabbed me by my shirt collar and pulled me close for a glorious kiss. For those of us old enough to remember, that moment was like the Love American Style! TV show of the 1970s, where couples kissed and fireworks filled the sky. Fate had delivered me an angel in 1984, and we've been together ever since.

By 1985, I had made a conscious decision that it was time for me to move on from Phone Programs and venture out on my own. My friends had nicknamed me "CMAD" by taking the first letter of my first name and combining it with the first three letters of my last name. I named my new company CMAD Communications.

It began with an old Smith-Corona electric typewriter, a desk, a couple of tape recorders, and a telephone just outside my bedroom in my father's home. My approach differed from Sports Phone's. Instead of one telephone hotline covering every sport, each service was dedicated to only one team and its related league. What was even more unique about this venture was that I did not charge the caller for the call itself. Instead, I gave it away but made up the production costs by selling advertisers on call volumes, marketing opportunities and total impressions in and around the building where the team played.

My very first client was the Chicago Blackhawks. And the Blackhawks Hotline was a hit! Soon, the Bears followed, as did the Chicago Cubs. Over the next several years, I eventually landed the Chicago White Sox and the entire National Football League.

But my big break came on a snowy winter's day in Chicago, in February of 1990. It was the night of Valentine's Day, and the city had been socked with about a foot-and-a-half of heavy, wet snow. I lived in Park Ridge, a suburb just outside the northwest tip of Chicago, and I had this long driveway, probably a good 20 yards long as did each of my neighbors.

When I woke up the next morning, I knew there was no way the snow blower would be able to cut through the thick stuff. So I began at 6:45 in the morning shoveling from just outside my garage door all the way into the front yard.

And I shoveled.

And I shoveled.

And I shoveled.

And when I completed my driveway and front walk, I assisted my next-door-neighbor, who had a heart condition, and did the same for him.

By the time I finished, it was about 4:30 in the afternoon, and I was drenched from snow and sweat. I walked in, peeled off my clothes, and looked down at the answering machine in the kitchen. The red light was flashing. I thought to myself, *Do I retrieve the messages or do I simply go upstairs and take a nice hot shower and settle in for a long winter's nap?* Thank goodness I pressed that button!

The voice of Lisa Seltzer, whom I had worked with at SportsChannel, echoed through the kitchen. "Chris, you're not gonna believe this, but the announcers from Molson Hockey Night couldn't make it in because of the bad weather, and we need a play-by-play announcer tonight to call the game at the Chicago Stadium between the Calgary Flames and the Chicago Blackhawks." I looked up at the clock—it was 4:40. She told me I needed to be there by 5:30. Clark Kent himself would have been envious of how quickly I showered and changed! I jumped in the car and somehow, despite the traffic and the icy road conditions, made it to the stadium on time.

There to greet me was Jacques Primeau, the director of the telecast. "Look, we couldn't get our announcers here, but we did get them back to our studios in Calgary. So, you're gonna do the first period. If you're struggling by the end of that period, we'll turn the broadcast over to them, and they can call it off the monitor."

I sat down and awaited the arrival of my partner and color analyst for the evening, the entertaining Harry Neale, who's a gem of a guy. We sat down and had a few moments to go over how we would manage our hand signals so we wouldn't step all over each other.

The showdown on ice began.

Names like Mike Keenan, Jeremy Roenick, and Doug Wilson instinctively rolled off my tongue. The chemistry between the color analyst and me was evident as Harry and I played off one another effortlessly. At least that's what I thought, but would the experts agree?

After the first period, a voice came over our headsets from the truck. It was Jacques Primeau. He was asked whether or not the talent back in the studio should take over for the remainder of the telecast. And Primeau said, "What? Are you kidding me? This kid is great! He's going the distance."

You could have peeled me off the ceiling! I felt sky high! With my confidence soaring, I had a strong call the rest of the game, along with one dynamite audition tape!

During the ride home, God's plan for my life began to register. In college, a hand injury forced me to the sidelines and into the radio booth. From there, I got a job at Sports Phone. That gave me the confidence to get involved with UIC Hockey. And now, a snowstorm had granted me my childhood wish to call a National Hockey League game.

As I turned up the driveway and set the car in park, I bowed against the steering wheel and thanked the good Lord above for all the opportunities He had blessed me with. Little did I know that my NHL journey had only begun.

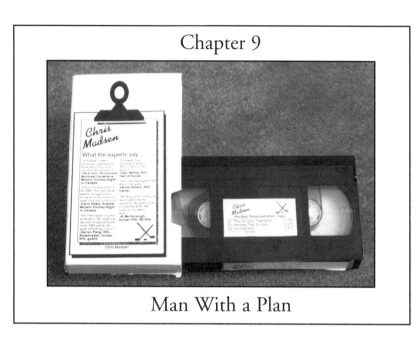

Chapter 9

Man With a Plan

Three years went by, and my business prospered. In 1993, the National Hockey League expanded to include the Mighty Ducks of Anaheim and the Florida Panthers based in Miami. Many times, my friends would ask, "Why don't you turn in a tape, Chris? You're just as good or better than those other guys."

I'd respond, "Well. Business is good. Life is good. Living in the suburbs is good. We're happy. I just don't think it's the time." But it was my wife Lori who insisted that I put together a tape just to see if there would be any interest.

I enlisted the help of one of the men I respect most in broadcasting, my partner from the mid-1980s, Bill Hazen, the very first man I had ever done a TV event with on SportsChannel-Chicago. Bill had become quite adept at tape and editing production. I showed him the Blackhawks/Calgary tape I had and gave him an idea of the kind of audition tape I wanted. I anticipated there would be several hundred people interested in the expansion teams' play-by-play jobs. I wanted to create a tape unlike any other that either the Mighty Ducks or the Florida Panthers would watch.

I had hired a TV crew for one evening to walk around the Chicago Blackhawks locker room and interview those players who were familiar with my work in Chicago and with the University of Illinois. I asked another friend, Rory Spears, if he would act as the interviewer, and I gave him these questions:

Tell me about Chris Madsen.

What do you think about Chris Madsen's call?

Do you think because he plays the game himself, it gives him a better feel for the game?

Is he ready to step up to the National Hockey League?

I had him approach three different people from the Blackhawks organization: Darren Pang, now an analyst with ESPN; Doug Wilson, who is presently the general manager of the San Jose Sharks; and E. J. Maguire, a former assistant coach with the Blackawks.

From the Blackhawks/Calgary game that I had announced that fateful snowy February night in 1990, I took the comments of Pang, Wilson, and Maguire and inserted them between highlights from that game.

One more marketing tool was added to my audition tape to help make it stand out from the rest. I manufactured a video box sleeve of personal recommendations. I contacted people with whom I had worked with over the years: Stan Mikita, a Hall of Fame center; Dick Irvin, Hall of Fame voice of the Montreal Canadiens; Harry Neale, my first ever NHL partner; Denis Savard, who had gone on to become a NHL Hall of Famer; Al McDonough, a former NHL All Star with the Pittsburgh Penguins, whom I had met at various adult hockey camps; and Darren Pang. Each was asked to deliver a one or two-line recommendation, something I could put on the box cover of my VHS cassette. On the plain side of some self-adhesive paper, Bill Hazen formulated what looked like a clipboard. We took each and every one of these comments and listed them one after another so that the person in Anaheim and Florida who opened the envelope would have something to read about Chris Madsen.

Talk about zillion-to-one shots. I had no agent. I had no inside contact at either team. And with that one exception, I had no National Hockey League game experience. But we put together a formula that we thought could work: a quick cut video that transitioned from pivotal moments in the Blackhawks/Calgary game with interspersed on-camera recommendations from Pang, Wilson, and Maguire to manufacturing a one-of-a-kind VHS box cover with the likes of Stan Mikita, Dick Irvin, Harry Neal, Denis Savard, Al McDonough, and Darren Pang selling Chris Madsen for—Chris Madsen!

Chapter 10

Chris Madsen

What the experts say...

"Articulate...comes prepared...a pleasure to work with. Chris is an excellent broadcaster!"
-Dick Irvin, Announcer, Montreal Canadiens, Molson Hockey Night in Canada

"Chris obviously follows the NHL. Not once did he fumble through rosters trying to locate a player's name. Great to work with!"
-Harry Neale, Analyst, Molson Hockey Night in Canada

"All Chris needs is a foot in the door. He could step into any broadcast booth in the NHL and do the game with flying colors!"
-Darren Pang, NHL Broadcaster, former NHL goalie

"I thought I was listening to Lloyd Pettit. Chris is that good."
-Stan Mikita, NHL Hall of Famer

"Asks intelligent questions. Knows the game."
-Denis Savard, NHL Center

"Working next to Chris, it was evident that he visualizes the game at an exceptional level. His calls are second to none."
-Al McDonough, former NHL All-Star

Chris Madsen

Making Contact

B efore I sent out the tapes, I contacted both clubs. My first call was to the Mighty Ducks of Anaheim. I reached Assistant Public Relations Director Rob Schicili, who explained to me, "You better get your tape in in a hurry. We have a stack of them already!"

I asked him for the names of the decision-makers in the selection process. He told me to contact the following: Ken Wilson, the VP of Broadcasting; Jack Ferriera, General Manager; and Tony Tavares, President and Alternate Governor. I asked to be transferred to Ken Wilson. Janet Conley, his administrative assistant, answered. What a stroke of luck this turned out to be because Janet was not only easy to talk to, but she also told me who should receive copies of my audition tape.

I was later told that when the tape arrived in Anaheim, Jack

Ferriera's administrative assistant, Barbara Potts, took the package and slit it open. She read the quotes on the box cover. Having once lived in the western suburbs of Chicago, Barb was immediately struck by Stan Mikita's quote that read, "Listening to Chris reminds me of Lloyd Pettit. He's that good."

As the story goes, she exclaimed, "If this guy sounds anything like Lloyd Pettit, he's our guy!" She immediately joined Jack Ferriera and Tony Tavares, and they viewed the tape in a nearby conference room. Barbara told me they ran about two minutes of the tape when Tavares said, "The search is over. We found our guy."

My tape went out in early July, and if I was their guy, the Ducks evidently were in no hurry to contact me.

I came home one day in August to prepare for an evening tennis lesson that my wife had set up when she said to me, "Some Duck called you."

I had been waiting for responses not only from Anaheim and Florida but also from New Jersey and Philadelphia. When she told me that some Duck had called, I thought she was trying to break the tension of our anxious evenings waiting for a response, and Lori had put a message of her own on the answering machine-something like "quack, quack, quack." Instead, it was Tony Tavares. His message went something like this, "Hello, Chris. This is Tony Tavares. I think you know what I'm calling about. Please get back to me as quickly as possible so we can talk."

With my heart in my throat, I found the number and called back. The two-hour time difference was in my favor. Tavares explained to me that he was in the process of nailing down the producer/director position and asked me about Lisa Seltzer, and I responded with a glowing recommendation. He asked about the business that I was involved in. He wanted to know what type of money I was looking for and how I would feel about making the transition from Chicago to the West Coast.

"We'd be all for it," I assured him.

Tavares said I could expect a follow-up phone call to set up an interview in the next couple of days. I thanked him, hung up the phone, and looked at my wife who had tears in her eyes. We walked over to the picture window, dropped to our knees, and prayed. Lori even said a little prayer to her devout Catholic grandmother who had passed away the year before. "Grandma Marge, please tug on the Big Man's sleeve and see if He can guide us to the West Coast." Our dear Lord was about to answer our prayers!

Chapter 11

Southern California, Here I Come!

A few days later, I received a phone call from Tony Tavares's administrative assistant, Sue Jackson. She arranged my airline and hotel accommodations. I called Terry and Barb Notko, friends of Lori and mine who had moved from Chicago to Laguna Hills in 1989, to tell them I was coming out to be interviewed about the play-by-play position with the Mighty Ducks.

Barb met me at John Wayne Airport.

"You have been paged for the last 15 minutes or so."

I picked up the white courtesy phone and was connected to Lori back in Park Ridge. She told me that Dean Jordan from the Florida Panthers had called and expressed an interest in talking to me about their play-by-play position and that he wanted to hear from me as soon as possible. I called Jordan, and he said he would call me on August 22 when I returned home from Anaheim.

As I hung up the phone, I stood in stunned disbelief. There I was in Orange County, California, to interview with the Mighty Ducks of Anaheim, and across the continent another team wanted to talk to me, too. *Somebody pinch me!*

Barb and I enjoyed a delicious dinner at an oceanfront restaurant in Huntington Beach. Before settling in at my hotel room at the Double Tree in Orange, I traveled over to take a look at the brand new arena that is now known as the Arrowhead Pond of Anaheim. As I looked at this magnificent structure, I just knew that this was going to be my "Field of Dreams."

Would Mr. Tavares make that dream come true?

Well, I'd have to get past the interview first.

The interview went something like this:

Tavares: So you think you're prepared for this interview?

Madsen: Absolutely.

Tavares: Good. Then can you produce a resume, 'cause I can't find the thing for the life of me.

Madsen: (Hands over resume.)

Tavares: Okay. I want you to pretend that you're interviewing me, but I want you to prove that you've done your homework. So, what I'm saying is I don't want any softball questions. I want the first question to prove to me that you came prepared. Now, I'm gonna count you down in 3, 2, 1, go.

Madsen: Hello, everybody. Welcome back to the Anaheim Arena. I'm joined now by the president and alternate governor of the Mighty Ducks of Anaheim, Tony Tavares. And you know what, Tony? I've scoured the past ten years of NHL yearbooks and media guides and not once in any team directory did I locate the name Tony Tavares. So, my opening question is, how does a guy with virtually no NHL team experience become the president of one of the most highly anticipated teams in NHL history?

Tavares: Now that's a great question (as Tavares proceeds to go into all the details about himself)!

Tavares: Okay. Now I have a question for you. Tell me about our head coach, Ron Wilson.

(Madsen delivers his response in great detail.)

Tavares: Now tell me about our assistant coach, Al Sims.

(Madsen again delivers his response in great detail.)

Tavares: All right. I'm gonna ask you about our other assistant coach. It's not really fair because he's relatively unknown, but do you know anything about Tim Army?

(Madsen had contacted Val Belmonte, a good friend and administrator at USA Hockey in Colorado, about Tim Army. Madsen proceeds to blow Tavares away with his detailed account of Army's background.)

Tavares: That's it. You've got the job!

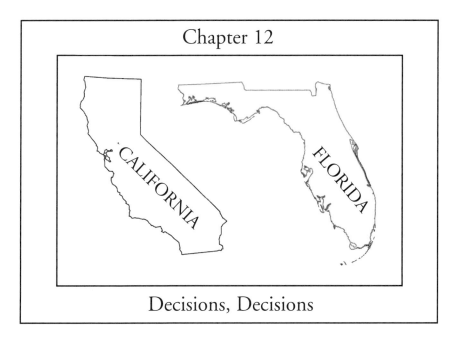

Chapter 12

CALIFORNIA

FLORIDA

Decisions, Decisions

Tony Tavares offered me the job, but I did not accept immediately. I first wanted to discuss the offer at length with my wife. Besides, Dean Jordan of the Florida Panthers was scheduled to call me that coming Saturday morning. I did not want to commit to anything yet.

Before leaving the Mighty Ducks offices, I called Lori and told her, "It's better than I anticipated." Tavares offered a three-year deal with the money fully guaranteed. Even though we hadn't discussed money past the first year, I knew that years two and three would simply be a formality.

As I mulled over the offer and crunched the numbers on the flight to Chicago, Lori apparently had already made up her mind. As I opened my front door, I saw streamers hung over the lamps, confetti on the floor, a chilled bottle of bubbly and champagne flutes on the dining room table. I held Lori close to me and said, "Well, maybe we shouldn't be celebrating just yet. We haven't heard what the Florida Panthers have to say."

"What?!?" Lori snapped.

Big mistake! I might as well have taken a pin and popped Lori's balloon.

The next morning, I spoke with Dean Jordan, Vice President of Broadcasting for the Florida Panthers. Florida seemed interested. The difference in the two potential offers was that the Panthers were considering a single-year deal with a limited number of games as an independent contractor. Since I was still running my company, being an independent contractor had a certain appeal. This would allow me to fly into Florida, call the game, fly back to Chicago, and continue to run my business.

Lori saw it differently. "Why would you possibly go for independent contractor status when you could be a full-time employee with full benefits and have the security of a three-year deal? And besides, it's always been my dream to be a *California* girl!" Lori was so frustrated with me that she marched out of the bedroom, locked herself in the bathroom, and claimed she wasn't coming out until we had a deal done in Anaheim.

I persisted, from my side of the bathroom door, with my counterargument that perhaps an independent contractor situation with Florida would grow year after year, allowing me to maintain my business in Chicago. I told her I was going to call our family attorney and friend, William Martin. Lori whined, "Oh, fine, you'll listen to your attorney, but you won't listen to your own wife."

With his always very persuasive delivery, Bill Martin walked me convincingly through this analogy. He said, "You remind me of the guy who's been wallowing in the minors, a rookie, looking for that first shot at the Bigs. You're sitting there with three bags of gold coins surrounding you, and yet you're going through each bag one by one, trying to see if there's a silver nugget tucked in there somewhere." He added, "Do the wise thing. Take the job in Anaheim. Take the security and grow with the franchise."

He convinced me. Or had he?

Chapter 13

Give Me A Sign, Dear Lord

Although we were leaning toward going to California, I needed some sort of assurance: a sign that this was the best decision. It had been over twenty-two years since my mother, Cecilia, had passed away from cancer, and it had been a difficult loss for me. I had yet to visit her grave since the day we laid her to rest.

I purchased some planting flowers and drove out to Elmwood Cemetery in Elmwood Park, Illinois. I stopped at the main office to get some assistance in finding my mother's headstone. A woman greeted me.

"How may I help you?" she asked.

"I'm looking for my mother's gravesite. Her name is Cecilia Madsen. 'M' as in Mary, 'a,' 'd' as in David, 's,' 'e,' 'N' as in Nancy."

"Here it is. She's located in Section 9. Just follow the main road halfway down, make a right at the reflection pond, take that road till it ends and make a left. You'll find your mother at the far east end of the cemetery, off the right-hand side of the road."

Her directions led me to a heavily shaded area near a majestic oak tree. I opened the trunk of the car and retrieved a watering can along with some gardening gloves and tools. Once I found her headstone, I started a long, overdue conversation with my mother.

"Hi, Mom. I want to apologize for not coming to see you sooner. I realize now how painful it is without you, and I sure do miss the heart-to-heart talks we used to have. I need to have one of those talks with you today, Mom. Life has afforded me a wonderful opportunity. Remember all those mock telecasts I used to stage with my Bobby Hull hockey game? You know, the ones where my screaming used to drive you and Dad crazy? Well, that dream may come true!

"You'd think I'd jump all over it, but it's not that easy. Lori will have to stay behind and help get the house sold. And leaving Dad and Nana behind is so hard. I know they're delighted for me, but I'll miss not being able to hop in my car and visit them.

"If you could just tug on the Big Man's coat sleeve and just give me a sign, and let me know that going to Anaheim is the right decision. You have no idea what it would mean to me."

And with that, I bowed my head and prayed. "Mom, please give us your blessing. Should Lori and I go to Anaheim?" I followed with the Lord's Prayer and sang softly as I had done so many times in church, *"Hear our prayer, O Lord. Hear our prayer, O Lord. Incline thine ear to us and grant us thy peace. Amen."*

When I lifted my head, the first thing I saw was the gravestone directly behind my mother's. It blared at me with big bold letters *D U C K*. As God as my witness, on that same headstone in the lower left-hand corner read "Ray M." My father's name is Raymond. I knew then that going to Anaheim to become the first ever television play-by-play voice in franchise history was my destiny.

"Thank you, Mom. I love you."

Chapter 14

Earning My Stripes

I returned to California. It was about three weeks from the first time I met with Tony Tavares. Lori stayed behind to sell our house in Park Ridge.

I learned that I wasn't just the television play-by-play announcer that first season—I was also pressed into duty with the Public Relations, Community Relations, and the Sales and Marketing Departments. Everyone in that front office got stretched, but nobody seemed to mind. The first year excitement was contagious, and everybody had this "What's next? What can I do?" type of attitude.

We were instructed to eliminate one word from our vocabulary. That word was "expansion." The front office felt that if its *cast members* used the word "expansion," it would become a built-in excuse for failure. We were a "new franchise," and that "new franchise" excitement took us a long way in year one; so far in fact that it set new NHL records for memorabilia sales, such as jerseys and jackets, T-shirts and hats.

But the Cinderella story didn't stop there. By mid-season, the Mighty Ducks were selling over 17,000 seats each game. This team of ragtag castoffs from every other club in the National Hockey League was also in the midst of setting an NHL record, with 33 victories in their first season, an incredible accomplishment.

I worked at honing my craft by studying videotape and taking heed of the advice shared with me by my peers. The performance bar was elevated in this television market. I was surrounded by some of broadcasting's giants—Vin Scully with the Los Angeles Dodgers, Chick Hearn of the L.A. Lakers, and Bob Miller, longtime voice of the L.A. Kings. Put them all together, and they had more than a century of broadcasting experience behind them.

On one occasion, a local sports reporter took aim at me and wrote: "When is Chris Madsen going to stop making every goal the Mighty Ducks score sound like a game-winning goal in Game 7 of the Stanley Cup Finals?"

The first time I read that, I wondered how Tony Tavares would respond. Tavares said, "You know what, Chris? If you can make every goal that we score sound like Game 7 of the Stanley Cup Finals, then do it because we're not going to Game 7 of the Stanley Cup Finals, at least just not yet."

When I read the newspaper quote to my father, his response was, "At least you know people are listening."

Well, I knew of at least one person who was listening consistently, and that was the unforgettable Joshua Souder.

Chapter 15

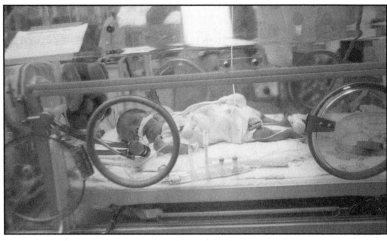

Miracle Baby

John and Robyn Souder longed to hear the "pitter patter of little feet" running through their home, but for years all they were greeted with was deafening silence. While living in York, Maine, the couple tried many times to start a family; however, the sad result was four miscarriages between 1980 and 1984. Robyn's doctor recommended that she undergo surgery to remove her right ovary, which was covered with cysts. Robyn and John thought seriously about adoption as an alternative. With just a week before her scheduled surgery, Robyn realized that her period was late. A blood test was ordered and came back positive. They were delighted and decided that if the baby were a boy, they would name him Joshua. Robyn chose the name Joshua because "he was Moses' right-hand man," and she wanted her son to be just as strong.

More than six months into the pregnancy, John and Robyn visited a little street fair in Portsmouth, New Hampshire. They came across a quaint bookstore and ventured inside. Mindful of her four previous miscarriages and the future of the baby inside her womb, a solemn desire overcame Robyn.

"While we're here, let's get a Bible," she said to her husband.

"Okay," John replied. "While we're at it, I'd like to get myself a cross."

Robyn spotted a Living Bible beautifully bound in burgundy leather with gold trim outlining the edge of each page. Meanwhile, John chose a jade carved cross and chain. Pleased with their purchases, they headed home.

Once they were home, did they open the Bible?

"Of course not," Robyn sheepishly confided.

Ten days later, at 28 weeks, 10 to 12 weeks premature, Joshua John Souder was born on Wednesday, July 4, 1984, at Portland Medical Center in Portland, Maine. Weighing just three pounds, two ounces and measuring only thirteen-and-a-half inches long, every breath little Joshua took, other than his first, was through the aid of a ventilator.

With his tiny chest heaving with every breath, doctors determined by 2 o'clock Thursday morning that Joshua's left lung had collapsed. A tube was inserted into his day-old chest cavity to relieve the air pocket between his lung and ribcage. Robyn admitted being "scared to death" to venture down the hallway to the Neonatal Intensive Care Unit. She was overcome with guilt because, "That was my child in there, and I was scared to death to see him." She had a special request of John. "Please bring me my Living Bible."

When John returned with Bible in hand, Robyn opened the book to its table of contents. Having grown up Catholic and a regular catechism attendee, Robyn considered herself well versed in the New Testament. But the Old Testament had a significant surprise in store for her.

As she scrolled down with her finger, she found the Books of

Genesis, Exodus, Leviticus, Numbers, Deuteronomy, Joshua. *Joshua!*

Oh my God! she thought. *I'm supposed to read this!*

In Joshua 1:6, Robyn was awestruck by the words: "Be strong and be brave. God is with you." Later that same morning, she shared her findings by phone with her mother, Maryann, and added verses 10 and 11, "Then Joshua issued instructions to the leaders of Israel to tell the people to get ready to cross the Jordan River. In three days, we will go across and conquer and live in the land which God has given us."

"Oh, well," Maryann assured her daughter, "then you have nothing to worry about. In three days, Joshua will get better."

On Friday, Joshua's condition took a catastrophic turn. As physicians struggled to bring his left lung back to health, Joshua's right lung collapsed. The combined lung failure forced Joshua's brain to overload and hemorrhage in the early hours of Saturday morning.

At 2:00 a.m., John was awakened by a phone call from one of Joshua's doctors asking that he return to the hospital immediately, adding that, "The prospects for your son are not good."

John raced back to the medical center to comfort his wife. Hope was fading as the doctors informed the Souders that Joshua's vital signs were weakening. His blood pressure was low, and his pulse was erratic, fluctuating from very slow to rapid, then back to slow. Another tube was threaded into the right side of Joshua's chest to relieve the pressure on his collapsed right lung; he needed constant assistance with breathing. Moreover, it would take a brain scan to determine the extent of the damage caused by the hemorrhage.

As Robyn and John approached the isolette to gaze upon their precious son, the nurses pulled out the tray that cradled Joshua's tiny body to offer the parents a soothing touch to say "hello," or perhaps a moment of contact before a long goodbye. Placing her right index finger inside of Joshua's tiny left hand, Robyn whispered, "Be strong, Joshua. Be brave. God is with you."

Joshua's skin was an ashy gray. His lips were a purplish blue. And his eyes were shut tight.

Joshua was in a fight for his life.

Together John and Robyn prayed to God to restore their son's vital signs. Minute by agonizing minute, as Joshua struggled, Robyn tried to read the doctors' body language. As they read Joshua's charts, a deep sigh and a shake of their heads from side to side confirmed Joshua's dire situation.

Standing beside his son, John gently removed the jade cross from around his neck and placed it atop Joshua's isolette.

"Be strong, Joshua. Be brave. God is with you, son."

Refusing to give up, Robyn kept reciting to Josh, "Every day in every way I'm getting better and better."

Within the hour, whatever Robyn and John were doing began to harvest results. As doctors returned every 10 to 15 minutes to check the monitors, they'd say, "Hmmm," leave the room, and return 10 to15 minutes later, and continue to look somewhat puzzled, yet hopeful.

Within an hour of making physical contact with his parents, doctors were so encouraged by the improvement in Joshua's vital signs that they ordered the nurses to slide Joshua back into the protective environment of the isolette. His miraculous recovery ended the deathwatch, a deathwatch that began on Thursday and ended on Saturday—three days, precisely as Scripture and Grandma Maryann had predicted.

But fragile Joshua was far from out of danger. Only a CAT (CT) scan could detect the extent of the brain damage the hemorrhage left behind and predict what challenges might lay ahead.

Meanwhile, emotional support arrived Saturday afternoon when John escorted his mother Jean, who had flown in from Riverside, California, into the room.

"Oh my gosh, Jean! It's so wonderful to see you!" Robyn exclaimed as all three embraced in a group hug.

"Well, I almost lost my job over coming out here. My boss tried to tell me that time off for family emergencies was limited to immediate family. So I told him, 'It's my grandchild. How much more immediate does it get?' So he says, 'If it's only your grandson, you can't go.' And I said, 'Oh yeah! Bet me!'" Grandma Jean's anecdote got a much-needed chuckle out of John and Robyn.

"Would you like to meet your grandson?" John asked.

"Absolutely."

John and Robyn guided Jean to the Neonatal Unit. They told her they'd give her some time alone with the newest member of the family and pointed her in the direction of the isolette off in the far left-hand corner of the room. Making her way past 12 other premies, Jean was overcome with emotion when she looked in on Joshua and "saw tubes everywhere."

Taking a moment to compose herself, Jean placed her hand on the protective plastic that separated her from her grandson and quietly said, "Hello Joshua. Grandma's here for you." A mother's instinct overtook Jean. She wanted to touch Joshua so desperately but didn't dare.

Suddenly, there was another voice in the room.

"He's the sickest one in the unit, you know?" a doctor offered.

"Oh, hello," a somewhat startled Jean responded. "Well, I know he's had quite an ordeal."

"Your children just don't appear to understand how serious their son's condition is."

"They're strong willed. In this case, they have to be. But you know? In spite of all the tubes, Joshua looks so healthy."

"Well, we'll know more when we get the results of the CAT scan."

With his vital signs holding steady, a CT scan was performed the next day.

On Monday, the pediatric neurologist entered Robyn's hospital room and pulled up a chair. Robyn, John and Jean sat on the bed holding hands hoping for the best.

"I want to begin by telling you that the news I have to share with you is not good. Your son has suffered a Grade 4 brain hemorrhage, and the damage is extensive. A Grade 4 is the worst kind, and he now has developed hydrocephalus, which is more commonly known as water on the brain. The long-term prognosis is not good either. He will most likely be a vegetable, and you may want to consider placing him in a home. He'll never know anyone or anything. He will never talk, walk, or even think. He will just be."

The Souders sat in stunned silence.

"You're wrong doctor. There's a light on in there," Robyn cried out. "I can see it!"

Still shaken by the news, the Souders tried to console each other, but Grandma Jean intercepted the doctor before he left. "If what you're saying is true, then why are you trying so hard to save him?"

"Because we have to," the doctor replied.

A defiant John exclaimed, "A vegetable? Not my son! Robyn, remember when we were stationed at the Royal Air Force Base in Lakenheath and we saw that story on hydrocephalus on the BBC? They said you could train the good parts of the brain to take over the mechanics of what the damaged parts are supposed to do."

"Yes," Robyn replied, "that's right!"

"Well, we're just going to have to work with Josh that much harder!"

A neonatologist quietly approached Robyn and John and whispered, "Don't believe everything the doctors tell you. Have hope and continue to pray." And they did.

From that moment forward, John worked vigorously on Joshua's arms and legs, and both parents kept a "You're my little tiger!" pep talk going. This ritual had begun during Robyn's pregnancy where every night she and John talked to and made reference to their little football player. The more John talked to his "little tiger" while he was in the womb, the more he'd kick. With his strong-willed parents behind him, Joshua's incredible journey was underway.

In his first year, Joshua had at least five revisions of a Ventricular Peritoneal shunt, which runs out of the third and fourth ventricles of his brain, along the side of his left ear, down the length of his neck, across his chest, and drains into his abdomen. The VP shunt acts as a type of plumbing system installed to help control pressure on the brain caused by hydrocephalus.

At two weeks, Joshua had heart surgery to close the petenductus valve in the heart, one that normally closes on its own. At 18 months, Joshua underwent surgery to correct his crossed eyes. At age three, tubes were inserted into both ears to combat infection. And at age five, Joshua had a selective dorsal rhyzotomy, which calls for the removal of the fifth vertebrae and electronically tests the spinal cord nerve bundles for spasticity.

By his parents' count alone, Joshua had beaten death three times.

Now, nearly 20 years and over 20 surgeries later, Joshua deals with spastic quadriplegic Cerebral Palsy. In layman's terms,

Joshua does not have the use of his right arm or both his legs. Those limbs are in a constant state of flex, which would be the equivalent of weight lifting the maximum amount of weights one possibly could, 24 hours a day. His arms and legs are so overwhelmed, they strain to manage.

Despite all they have gone through and go through today, the Souder family considers it a blessing. In the words of Grandma Jean, "Without God's hand, it would not have happened. Some divine presence intervened."

Grandma Maryann presented Robyn and John with a piece of white paper. Typed on the paper was the following poem that would serve as a constant reminder of the beautiful gift they had been blessed with.

Heaven's Very Special Child

A meeting was held quite far from earth.
"It's time again for another birth."
Said the angels to the Lord above,
"This special child will need much love."
His progress may seem very slow.
Accomplishments he may not show.
And he'll require extra care
From the folks he meets way down there.
He may not run or laugh or play.
His thoughts may seem quite far away.

In many ways he won't adapt.
And he'll be known as handicapped.
So let's be careful where he's sent.
We want his life to be content.
Please, Lord, find the parents who

Will do a special job for You.
They will not realize right away
The leading role they're asked to play.
But with this child sent from above
Comes stronger faith and richer love.
And soon they'll know the privilege given
In caring for this gift from heaven.
Their precious charge, so meek and mild,
Is heaven's very special child!

By Edna Massimilla (c) 1956
Reprinted with permission by
This Is Our Life Publications for Disabled
P.O. Box 21
Hatboro, PA 19040

Chapter 16

"You Can Do That!"

Grandparents can make such a wonderful impact in a child's life. In my family, my nana's promise to my mother that she would help our father raise us, I'm convinced, made it possible for my mother to go in peace, as well as provided us with positive memories and values.

In Joshua's family, his two grandmothers, Jean and Maryann, played a significant role, not only in those early days and months and years, but continuing until this day. Because of his premature birth, Joshua would always be behind schedule physically. At the suggestion of some of the nurses, Robyn and John considered dressing Joshua in Cabbage Patch Doll clothes. But at three months, even these clothes were too big!

Grandma Maryann to the rescue! In the tradition of grandmothers, Maryann took needle and thread and fashioned three custom-made outfits for Joshua. The first was a beautiful miniature white-flowing christening gown and bonnet. The second was a turquoise soccer jersey with a ball on the front and Joshua's name on the back. And the last became one of Joshua's favorites, a red baseball jersey with white pinstripes and sleeves.

If there was one thing Joshua responded to as an infant, it was baseball. Grandma Jean had presented Joshua with one of his first gifts—a plush white baseball with red sewn-on seams. By the time Joshua turned one, he could easily distinguish this gift from all others.

John and Robyn would sit across the room from Joshua and line up a football, a soccer ball, a basketball, and his plush baseball. At their signal, Joshua would begin to "combat crawl," propelling himself forward with his elbows and knees, over to his prized possession.

Both parents awaited Joshua's first word. Mothers hope it will be "Mama," while fathers hope for "Dada."

The first word that one-year-old Joshua Souder, present-day aspiring sports broadcaster, ever uttered was "ball."

Baseball became his passion. At age six, Robyn and John signed him up for Challenger Baseball. This program provides an opportunity for children with disabilities to play the game they love. Joshua's favorite position was third base. If a ball was hit in his direction, the buddy fielder would glove it and hand it off to Joshua, who would wind up left handed and fire the ball over to first base.

Challenger Baseball became a family affair for the Souders: John coached, Robyn managed, and Sarah, Josh's younger sister, helped out in the field. Although the game was designed to play off a batting tee, John was determined that every challenged child, including his son, would learn how to hit a pitched ball. Joshua practiced hard and eventually mastered his single-handed swing technique.

Baseball is Joshua's passion off the field as well. He enjoys listening to broadcaster Vin Scully. At eight, Josh, while watching a televised Dodgers baseball game, declared to his mother, "I want to be a sportscaster."

Prior to this declaration, Joshua had talked about becoming a policeman or fireman. But his parents had thought the physical demands of both these professions would eliminate Joshua as a candidate. *But a sportscaster?* Robyn thought to herself. *You can do that!*

Oh, he could do it all right. But it would cost Mom some money.

Joshua made an appeal to his mother to go along with his newfound vocation. "Can we get the newspaper delivered?" he asked. Robyn, now a single mom following her divorce from John, was counting pennies just to put food on the table. But she found a way to make Joshua's request a reality.

Every morning, Joshua excitedly tore through the paper to locate the sports section.

Funny, Robyn thought to herself, *the little stinker needs the print on his homework enlarged, but he's having no trouble reading the sports page!*

After meeting me, Robyn said she really noticed an increase in her son's appetite for sports information. Joshua has become so adept, that all he needs to hear from the television broadcaster is a few syllables, and he can identify the announcer, the site, the home team, and the road team.

On family trips to Anaheim or Los Angeles, Joshua used to sing Gospel hymns. Now, he conducts mock broadcasts.

"Live from Chavez Ravine, FOX Sports Net presents Dodger Baseball!" Josh calls out from his backseat perch in the family van. Joshua's parents respond with words of encouragement from the front seat.

This "can-do" spirit is what motivates Joshua Souder and inspires others. The word "can't" has been eliminated from his vocabulary. Ask Joshua what C.P. stands for, and he'll tell you, "Most people think it stands for Cerebral Palsy, but I think it stands for Capable Person!"

Chapter 17

The Pleasure Was Ours!

I had promised nine-year-old Joshua at FanFair that I would get him tickets to see his first ever Mighty Ducks game. Hoping to make it a special experience for him, I huddled together with Ducks defenseman David Williams and his wife, Pam. We agreed to pool each other's pair of tickets in exchange for four together in the lower level disabled seating area. After checking the season schedule, the final home game of the inaugural season was on April 13 versus the Vancouver Canucks. The fact that the game wasn't televised allowed me the optimum time to spend with my special friend.

As the Souder van pulled up to the Arrowhead Pond of Anaheim, the side door rolled back to unveil an automated chair lift. Joshua expertly maneuvered his wheelchair into position and slowly began his dissent to the pavement below.

Joshua looked as cute as ever with his curly blond hair

peeking out from beneath a purple and jade paneled Mighty Ducks cap. He sported a close-fitting gray Mighty Ducks sweatshirt and some loose fitting blue jeans that concealed the braces that held his legs firmly against his electric wheelchair. With an ear-to-ear grin, gleaming eyes, and his left hand extended, Joshua initiated high fives and hugs all around for Pam, Lori, and myself.

Once we settled into our seats in Section 204, I pulled up a chair next to Joshua and presented him with the announcer's "bible"—a copy of the Mighty Ducks Media Guide along with a press kit for the evening's event. These items are a play-by-play announcer's lifeblood in terms of on-air preparation. With his tiny left hand, Joshua began thumbing through the notes like a seasoned pro.

"How do you pronounce this guy's name?" Joshua inquired while pressing a finger next to the name of number 29, Randy Ladoucer.

"La-du-sir," I answered phonetically. "Try it with me, Josh?"

"Number 29, Randy La-du-sir," we announced in unison.

For the next three hours, Joshua and I called the action like a mock broadcast.

"Here comes Terry Yake down the wing, shooting! Just wide! What do you think, Josh?" I asked trying to get a rise out of my "Broadcasting Booth Buddy."

"I think we've got to put the puck on net. That's what I think," Josh shot back like a veteran analyst.

Incorporating game notes, Josh asked, "Hey Chris? Did you know that Captain Troy Loney won a Stanley Cup with the Pittsburgh Penguins?"

We shared cotton candy in between sound bites. Like two kids in a candy store, we had the time of our lives. I looked on in wonderment at this brave, challenged little boy who was

somehow able to put his cares and troubles on the shelf and realized that my cares and troubles are comparatively insignificant
and fleeting.

Lori commented, "I don't know who's having more fun, you
or Josh."

In unison, Josh and I answered, "I am!"

Robyn remembers the events that took place at that game
vividly. In her private memoirs, Robyn writes:

> *Because it was not a televised game, we had the honor of
> having Chris spend the entire game sitting next to Joshua
> leaning on his wheelchair, giving him private play-by-play
> action. Chris, being a popular, polite celebrity, had many
> people coming by to see him during the game. The first words
> out of his mouth on each new encounter were, "I would like
> you to meet my friend, Joshua Souder." He never once forgot
> that he was sitting with Joshua.*
>
> *After giving Joshua several Ducks items—a hat auto-
> graphed by all the players was one of the items—he took us
> down to the locker room to meet all the players. As we wait-
> ed outside the door of the locker room, and as each player
> came out, Chris would introduce them to Joshua and ask
> them to sign a poster that Joshua had laying on the tray of his
> wheelchair. As each player leaned over the tray to sign the
> poster, Chris would pat them on the back, thanking them for
> their time and for signing. It was as if Joshua was his child,
> and he cared more than words can say.*
>
> *When [head coach] Ron Wilson came out of the locker
> room, he stopped to talk with Joshua also. One of the things
> that Joshua had prided himself on learning was all the NHL
> teams, their cities, and the arenas that they play at. Ron start-
> ed quizzing Joshua and then tricked him by asking about the
> minor league teams. Joshua got a big laugh out of that one.*

> *But the last player to come out was [goaltender] Guy
> Hebert. He spoke to Joshua for just a minute or two before
> he said, "I don't suppose you would like a goalie stick to hang
> on your wall, would you?" Joshua's jaw dropped open with
> astonishment. Guy autographed his stick and gave it to him.
> As I stood there dumbfounded, Chris was thanking him,
> again as if Joshua was his own child.*
>
> *At the end of that evening, it was very difficult for us to
> sleep. It was as if we were on a natural high for days. We had
> never met so many people who were so kind. The whole
> Ducks organization was full of people with big hearts. We
> even had the opportunity to meet Michael Eisner, who asked
> Joshua if he was going to be back next year. He was also a
> very nice man.*

Robyn later recalled how she, Joshua and his friend, Josh
Millsap, were "buzzed" from a natural high and didn't come
down until they went to bed around 2:30 in the morning. When
Laura Millsap arrived later that day to pick up her son, Robyn
and the boys were still carrying on.

"It was just a magical night," Robyn told Laura. "If you
weren't there, I could see why it'd be hard to understand."

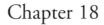

Chapter 18

More Challenges

In November of 1994, Joshua's head was buzzing once more, but this time for all the wrong reasons. As Thanksgiving approached, Joshua had developed severe headaches, many times accompanied by nausea and vomiting. By mid-December, doctors determined that Joshua's shunt was malfunctioning. On December 17, "the poor soul," as his mother many times referred to him during his times of crises, was given some relief following surgery. Unfortunately, as it was to be with many of his surgeries, this relief was only temporary.

By early April, the symptoms started again. This time they were accompanied by lethargy. On April 4, doctors at Loma Linda Children's Hospital repeated the surgery they had performed in December. Joshua's recovery was so swift that he was able to play Saturday Challenger baseball only three days later.

However, by Sunday, he was running a temperature.

Eight days later, Joshua underwent a second brain surgery. Because an infection had developed, he was fitted with an external shunt and was placed in the Intensive Care Unit for the next ten days. Confident that all signs of infection had subsided, Joshua had two additional procedures on April 22: first, the removal of the external shunt, followed by the insertion of another internal system.

Once again, shortly after this procedure was completed, Joshua began to suffer the same ill effects: severe headaches, nausea, vomiting. This time there was an added twist: short-term memory loss.

Joshua asked his mom and dad, "Where is my sister?" They pointed Sarah out to him. No sooner had they done so, Joshua asked the same question.

Following surgery three days later to place a "Y" connector in Joshua's Ventricular Perotoneal shunt, a critical device that regulates the spinal fluid drainage from both the right and left ventricles of the brain, Robyn was informed that no one, including parents, is allowed to sleep in an Intensive Care Unit room during the night. She was given a pillow and sheet and a place to sleep in a general waiting area. Ever resourceful, she fashioned a bed by placing a pair of ottomans side by side in the corner of the room. Exhausted, Robyn drifted off to sleep—but not for long.

At 5:30, Robyn sprung up from her makeshift sleeping quarters convinced that something was terribly wrong with Joshua. She quickly gathered her things and raced down the hallway towards the ICU. The instant she charged into the room, she locked eyes with her son.

"Mom, help me, please! It's my head! My head!"

Gently lifting Joshua's head, Robyn saw that the dressing and pillow were drenched with sweat.

"Let Mommy wash her hands, and we'll get you comfy."

As Robyn turned to enter the washroom, Joshua screamed, "My head!" and projectile vomited on the pillow, bed and floor. Robyn switched on the intercom and paged the nurse.

"Mommy, something's wrong! I don't feel well at all."

"That's it! I'm calling your father."

John was home getting Sarah ready for school when Robyn telephoned him. "Robyn, I'll get there as quickly as I can."

Robyn wet a washcloth and began to dab away at her son's face. She noticed that what she thought was sweat on her fingers felt somewhat odd. She lifted Joshua's head again and cried out, "Oh my God! Honey, I'm going to get a doctor."

The nurse charged into the room, and Robyn instructed her to "Get a doctor, quick!"

"What's wrong?"

"Look! This isn't natural. Look at his head. It's saturated!"

"Oh, that's just cirrus drainage, which is common after surgery."

"Cirrus drainage? Not this much! I want a doctor to see him right now!"

"My head is killing me, Mommy," Joshua interrupted. "Something's wrong with my head."

The nurse clicked on the intercom. "Get a pediatric neurosurgeon to Unit 5700 Stat!"

Within minutes, the doctor rushed through the doorway. "What seems to be the problem?" he inquired, taking hold of Joshua's wrist.

Lifting Joshua's head once more, Robyn demanded, "Doctor, will you please look at this?" as she exposed Joshua's saturated bandage.

He examined the 3-inch incision behind Joshua's left ear and ordered an immediate CT scan. And, alarmed, he said, "And his pulse is 45."

"What is it?" Robyn asked.

"It appears to be spinal fluid. We've got to act now!"

The doctor and an orderly placed Joshua on a gurney and ran with him down the hallway. Robyn paced the room like a caged animal. She stopped in mid-stride met by John who turned the corner and questioned, "Where's Josh? Is he all right?"

"They're performing a CAT scan, and we should be getting the results any moment now. Who's going to pick up Sarah?"

"Don't worry. Mom is," John said as he gently cradled Robyn in his arms.

Several minutes passed, but they seemed like hours as John and Robyn held hands waiting for the verdict.

The pediatric neurosurgeon tapped lightly on the open door.

John and Robyn inquired in unison, "Doctor, can you tell us what's wrong?"

"The Y-connector implanted yesterday appears to be malfunctioning. The spinal fluid level in Joshua's left ventricle is too low, and the level in his right ventricle is too high. When the fluid is too low, the ventricle collapses, and if it gets even lower, the chamber collapses, and that could trigger a number of things and could prove fatal. If the ventricle is too full, the chamber swells and puts enormous pressure on the brain."

Welling up with tears, Robyn asked, "So what you're saying, Doctor, is that my son could die?"

"Yes. But I think I can correct it."

"Please, Doctor," John pleaded, "by all means, take care of our son."

"I'll do my best."

"One more question," Robyn injected.

"Yes?"

"If all goes well, how long should this surgery take?"

"About two hours."

"May we see him before you start?"

"Certainly."

As they wheeled Joshua into the operating room for the fifth time inside a month, on the morning of May 3, 1995, Robyn recited her familiar conviction, "Be strong and be brave. God is with you."

John reminded himself as he looked down at his beautiful son to never say good-bye, knowing that whenever someone had done so in the past, Joshua would burst into tears. Instead, John garnered all his inner strength, leaned forward and whispered into his son's ear, "See you in a bit, Tiger."

Going on seven hours after surgery, ten-year-old Joshua Souder lie in his recovery room bed officially listed as comatose. Two tall stools were brought into the room so Robyn could comfortably hold Joshua's right hand and stroke his hair while Pastor John Douglas from the family's Crossroads Christian Church in Corona cradled his left hand.

Normally, Josh was responsive and a "chatterbox" coming out of surgery, but not this time.

Robyn kept John, who returned home to tend to Sarah, and the rest of the extended family abreast of Joshua's condition by phone.

Robyn's mother, Maryann, tried to console her daughter by saying, "If God decides to bring him home . . ."

Robyn interrupted her mother in mid-sentence screaming, "How dare you even say something like that!"

"All I'm saying, Robyn, is that if Josh should pass, he won't be in anymore pain. You must prepare yourself."

Maryann's motherly advice began to sink in. Robyn thought to herself, *She must see the worst, too, because normally she's so positive.*

As Robyn leaned forward, through her tears she whispered into her son's ear, "Be strong and be brave. God is with you." And with that the phone rang.

Chapter 19

The Greatest Call I Ever Made

The National Hockey League plays an 82-game regular season schedule that is usually completed by the second week in April. During the 1994-95 season, or what has come to be known as the '95 season, that was not the case. A labor dispute between the owners and the players resulted in a lockout that eventually cost both sides the first three-and-a-half months of the season. Once a new Collective Bargaining Agreement was reached, both sides agreed to play an abbreviated 48-game season that was to begin the third week of January and end the first week of May.

Hoping to continue our budding "tradition" of bringing Joshua back for the final game of the season, I called the Souder residence. No one answered, so I left a detailed message on their answering machine.

"Hello, Souders! This is Chris Madsen. I've made arrange-

79

ments for the four of you to be my guests at the season finale against Toronto on May third at 7:30. I'll leave the tickets under Joshua's name at the concierge desk. I've also made special parking arrangements. Enter on the backside of the building through the far left-hand parking booth that's designated *Media*. The tickets will be available anytime after 6:30. Please call me back to confirm."

I anticipated a swift and enthusiastic reply.

A few days passed, and on the afternoon of our final game of the season, I tried again. Everything was in place except for Joshua and his family. Once more, the answering machine greeted me. I left a last-ditch message.

"Hi! This is Chris again. I left you a message a couple of days ago regarding tonight's game. I can hold the tickets until 5:30 today. If I don't hear back from you by then, I'll assume you can't use them, and I'll pass them along to someone else. I hope everything's all right, and that I'll see you tonight."

Unlike Joshua's season-ending visit the previous year, I had to prepare for a telecast. Time was getting tight, and just before five o'clock, I had to voice over some sponsorship billboards, conduct a pre-taped interview, and look over the copy I would read that evening during natural stoppages in play. By 5:30, I was back at my desk. No sooner did I settle into my chair, then the phone rang. It was Joshua's father.

"Chris, Joshua's in bad shape."

My heart jumped into my throat. "What's wrong?" I asked.

"He's in the ICU at Loma Linda. Robyn's there."

"How bad is he, John?"

"He's in a coma."

"A coma?"

"Chris, if you have a moment, Robyn would really like to talk to you."

"Certainly."

My heart sank as I wrote down the telephone number John gave me. My stomach was in knots.

"Look, I've got to get back to the hospital, but please call Robyn."

"You have my word."

I hung up the phone, stood up, and took a series of deep breaths in an attempt to compose myself before making the call to Robyn. Sitting back down, I thought to myself, *What do you say to a mother whose precious young son is in peril?* One ring, and Robyn was on the line.

"Hello, Robyn."

"How's my 'Broadcasting Booth Buddy'?"

"Not good, I'm afraid."

Those four words momentarily took my breath away. An ominous foreboding tugged at my spirit, and my eyes began to well up.

Robyn explained, "The poor little soul has been through so much Chris. He almost died. . . ." She was barely able to choke out those words. "I'm sorry, Chris, but it's so hard to see him like this."

"You have nothing to be sorry about. This is your son's life."

"I've been here for hours stroking his hair, holding his hand, talking to him. Pastor Douglas has been talking to him, too. We just can't get any response from him. I've spent most of the day praying to God that He doesn't take my son."

"And He's listening, Robyn. Believe me, He's listening. Robyn, is there anything, anything at all, that I can do?"

"Chris, we've tried just about everything," she said, her voice cracking. "But wait. How about if I put the phone by his ear? Would you say a few words to him? I believe he can hear us, but he's just not responding. Perhaps if he hears your voice, it'll make a difference."

"Okay, I'll give it a try," I said anxiously. But before I had time to think of what I might say, I could hear the bedclothes rustling as Robyn placed the phone next to Josh's ear. I could also hear my heart pounding in my ears.

"Okay," Robyn whispered, "go ahead."

Feeling a bit apprehensive, I began with the obvious. "Hey, Joshua, this is Chris Madsen."

No response.

Straightaway, I decided to talk in a language Joshua could understand and appreciate—sportscaster lingo. "Well, Josh, tonight the Mighty Ducks close out their 48-game schedule against the Toronto Maple Leafs. The Ducks, who have lost three straight, will start Mikhail Shtalenkov in goal."

Again, there was no response.

My apprehension increased, but I kept on, "If the Ducks pull off a victory tonight, they'll finish the season with a record of 16 wins, 27 losses, and 5 ties good for 37 points."

I waited, feeling the tension building in my throat.

"Now, Josh, don't forget to join us for all the action beginning at 7:30 on KCAL-9. Remember to tell the nurses you want to watch the Ducks versus the Maple Leafs on Channel 9 at 7:30."

Nothing. Dreadful silence.

I paused to collect my thoughts. I began to pray a simple but direct prayer. *Dear God, please help me reach this little boy!* Just that quickly, a familiar battle cry dawned on me. Invigorated with a renewed sense of hope, I continued, "You know what, Joshua? If I was in that room right now, I'd lean way over that bed, and I'd put my mouth right up next to your ear, and I'd call out, **'Joshua shoots! He scores! Ducks win!'"**

I heard movement.

Then Robyn cried out, "Oh my God!" in the background. The sound I was hearing was Joshua reaching over with his left hand, rolling over on his right side, and bringing the receiver up to his mouth.

"Hello, Chris! How are you?" he bellowed.

The sound of his voice pierced straight through me. "Joshua? Is that you?"

"Yes!"

"You're asking *me* how *I* am? How are you?" I asked as tears streamed down my face.

I heard Robyn in the background, "It's a miracle! It's a miracle! My baby's back! It's a miracle!" Pastor John Douglas clapped his hands. The celebration was on! Robyn ran out and yelled at the stunned nurses, "He's talking! He's talking! He's talking on the phone!"

John ran down the hallway to see what all the commotion was about. Chatterbox Joshua was back!

"I promise to tune in tonight at 7:30," Joshua declared, proof that even while Joshua was "out" he was tuning in!

"I'll try to sneak in a 'hello to you, little buddy' if I get a chance," I vowed.

"That would be awesome!" Joshua replied.

"Joshua?"

"Yes, Chris?"

"I just wanted to tell you how much I love you."

"I love you too, Chris."

"Your mom and your dad and your sister and your grandparents and all your friends—do you realize how much they love you?"

"Yes."

"All of our prayers have been answered, Josh. I love you, little buddy. God bless you, Josh. Thanks for coming back."

"Thank you, Chris!"

"I'll see you in the booth, okay?"

"Okay."

"Now let me talk to your mother."

"Mom, Chris wants to talk to you."

An ecstatic Robyn got back on the line as I pushed back more than a few tears of joy from my eyes.

"Well, Robyn, our prayers have been answered!"

"Have they ever!"

"It looks like I'll be getting you tickets for next year," I said, trying to add some levity.

Through her tears she chuckled, "Who cares about next year? You've given me back my son! Thanks to you and thanks to God, my son is back! It's a miracle!"

"Josh is the miracle, Robyn. Josh is the miracle."

John later admitted that when he came to the hospital that day, he expected the worst. "I had almost lost all hope at that point," he confessed. "I remember thinking, *How do you prepare yourself for something like this?* That thought went through my head a lot, and talking to Robyn, I could tell she was thinking about it, too. We prayed for a miracle, and one came through."

By the way, the Ducks won the game, 6 to 1.

Chapter 20

Joshua, MVP

"Doctors will tell you that it takes a child's body six months to heal from surgery," Robyn once told me. One could only imagine how much healing Joshua had ahead of him. The process was slow but steady. Joshua passed the time by becoming quite proficient at whipping all challengers at Yahtzee! and Cribbage. Joshua's delicate condition, the demands of a National Hockey League schedule and the miles between us made it difficult to get together. But there was always the mail! And Joshua loves getting mail! An occasional letter was met with sheer delight. To me, Joshua Souder is a daily slice of Christmas—bright, colorful, and full of love. I shared the following with him in a letter dated January 3, 1996:

Dear Josh:

Just got off the phone with a mutual friend of ours, Bart

Lucente, and he gave me the terrific news that you're feeling much, much better. Bart also told me that you have returned to school. Fantastic!

The last time we talked, you told me that "a good dose of hockey" would make you feel better. So, after you get all caught up on your homework, snuggle up with your mom and sister in front of the television and get ready to relive all the excitement of your favorite team's spectacular inaugural season . . . with your favorite announcer calling the action! (ha! ha!)

Josh, people ask for so many things around this time of year. I'm convinced your recovery has provided all the people who love and care about you so very much, with the greatest possible gift.

Thank you for my gift. Proving once again, "Joshua Shoots. He Scores" every time!

> *Your friend and Broadcasting*
> *Booth Buddy,*
>
> *Christopher M. Madsen*
> *Play-by-play*
> *Television Announcer*

Letters of faith and friendship were critical to Joshua's recovery. His spirit soared!

Academically and socially, there was no slowing Joshua. He graduated from Riverview Elementary in 1997. He earned a special certificate for the most years of service ever by a student. He breezed through Norco Intermediate, graduating in 1999. At Santiago High School in Corona, California, Joshua became one of the "Big Men on Campus." I likened walking the school grounds with Joshua to being alongside the mayor of Corona.

Everywhere he went, his friends and schoolmates would call out, "Hi Joshua!"

"Hello!" Joshua would shoot back accompanied by an appreciative wave of his left hand.

Three times Joshua was voted the Most Valuable Person on Campus. For four straight years, the varsity football team, recognizing that Josh rarely missed a Santiago Sharks game, presented him with the Number 1 Fan Award. He earned three varsity letters for academics, was voted a prince in the 2002 Homecoming Court, and served for four years as manager and public address announcer for the high school basketball team. The 2002-2003 basketball season was dedicated to Joshua, and for the first time in school history, a jersey was retired in his honor.

But just how true to his school is Joshua Souder? I had made arrangements with Tim Ryan, the general manager of the Arrowhead Pond of Anaheim, to extend to Josh and his family a luxury suite for a Friday night Mighty Ducks home game. Joshua politely declined my invitation but asked for a rain check because the Sharks had a football game and he wasn't about to break his consecutive-games-watched streak. Being in the midst of a consecutive-games-broadcast streak with the Ducks myself, I told him I thoroughly understood.

But on the night of the game torrential rains and high winds swept through Southern California, and all I could do was think of Joshua. Prior to going on the air that night, I telephoned him. Since we had last talked, he had come down with flu-like symptoms. I tried to convince him that no streak was as important as his health.

"Okay," he acquiesced, not at all convincingly.

His dad later told me that just before kickoff, Joshua pleaded with his parents to take him to the game. Joshua's streak would remain intact. Unfortunately, the contents of his stomach did not!

John said that Joshua vomited at the game and continued to vomit all the way home.

But, most importantly to Josh, he didn't miss the game!

His unwavering dedication and loyalty to the school made Joshua the logical choice to receive the 2002 Corona-Norco Coalition of Community Groups Award, United Neighbors Involving Today's Youth (UNITY).

For four years, Joshua's "neighbor" at the lunch table was Santiago High School Varsity Women's Basketball Coach Jim Le Duc. Between bites, Josh and Jim forged a very special friendship and a mutual admiration for one another that inspired Coach Le Duc to write the following poem:

The Hero of the Game

If only I made that free throw,
If I hit just one more three,
If I wouldn't have missed that board,
If I just played better "D,"
Then I wouldn't drop my head in shame
'Cause I'd be the hero of the game.

If the refs didn't make that call,
If my leg wasn't so sore,
If my teammates would pass the ball,
If a decent crowd would ever show,
Then I'd make myself a name
'Cause I'd be the hero of the game.

If coach would call a better play,
If my shoes weren't so old,
If that noisy fan would go away,
If I didn't have this darn cold,

Then I'd build up quite the fame
'Cause I'd be the hero of the game.

There will always be another excuse
That someone as great as me can use
To point anywhere else the finger of blame
To justify why I'll never be the hero of the game.

* * * * *

I'd make that free throw!
I'd nail that three!
I'd get that board!
I'd shut 'em down with "D!"
'Cause in my wheelchair, I feel no shame
When in my dreams, I'm happy just to play the game.

I wouldn't mind the ref's call,
I could handle my legs being sore.
I would pass my teammates the ball,
I would appreciate any fan to show.
'Cause if I could just walk and not be lame,
Then I'd be so honored just to play the game.

I would run any of coach's plays,
I wouldn't mind playing in shoes that are old.
I don't care if that noisy fan stays,
I can play through this little cold.
'Cause if just for a moment, God could straighten
*   my frame,*
My ultimate dream would come true—to just play
*   the game.*

If we ever think to give an excuse
When we reflect on the talents God gave us to use,
The only man worthy to point a finger of shame
Is Joshua Souder, the real hero of the game!

Reprinted with permission by
Jim LeDuc (2002)

Santiago High School's motto is "Home of Scholars, Achievers, and Champions." Joshua Souder is the embodiment of all three attributes and then some, similar to another hero in my life.

Chapter 21

I Miss You, Dad

The record may show that my dad, Raymond Joseph Madsen, was not a scholar. But it will show him as an achiever and certainly as a champion to his family and friends. My dad was my compass, and he meant the world to me. I am the youngest of three children and had the luxury of sitting in the back row and marveling at my dad and my nana, his mother-in-law, as they stepped up to the plate after my mom passed away on May 12, 1971. This was no easy task when you consider that Dad had to play both father and many times mother to sixteen-year-old Karen, Marc in the middle at fourteen, and me pulling up the rear at twelve. These were not exactly easy phases in our lives for two parents to handle, let alone one. But my dad did so magnificently. And although there may have been posters of Hall-of-Famers Johnny Bench, Joe Namath, and Stan Mikita on my bedroom walls, from that point forward if anyone would ask, my dad was my idol. But boy, I wished he'd quit smoking.

By the spring of 1983, Dad had developed a nasty morning smoker's cough. Day after day, morning after morning, Dad kept hacking away. On my way to work one day, I stopped to fill 'er up at the gas station my family frequented. The owner stopped me and said, "Man, I saw your dad in here yesterday, and he looked awful." That thought stuck with me throughout my ride to my offices in downtown Chicago at the John Hancock Center. Once inside, I broke down. My boss told me to go home for the day, and when my father, who rarely missed a day's work, found out that I was sent home because of his condition, he decided to make an appointment for a complete physical.

Dr. Robert Head ordered a lung x-ray straight away, and shortly thereafter located a cancerous tumor the size of a golf ball in the upper lobe of my dad's right lung. Dr. Head planned on removing a section of the lung through an incision made just below the right shoulder blade. But once he opened up my father, he decided to take no chances and removed the entire right lung.

When he delivered the news to my family, we were stunned. When he delivered the same news to my father and suggested that he begin treatments with an oncologist, my dad asked, "You think you got all of it?"

"Yes," the doctor replied.

"Then that's good enough for me. I saw what chemo and radiation did to my wife, so I'll take my chances. When can I go back to work?" he asked.

"In two to three months, you can begin to ease your way back in, Ray."

"I'll be easing my way back in in three to four weeks."

Actually, we started dropping Dad off at his office three-and-a-half weeks after surgery. He'd stay for an hour or two to gradually build his way back.

My dad is an unforgettable soul. When I told my dad that I had nailed down the job in Anaheim, he rushed out to the local J.C. Penney and cleaned them out of every Mighty Ducks T-shirt and sweatshirt they had. He handed those things out like a new father doles out cigars.

At the tail end of our inaugural season, something very strange happened to me. I suddenly felt nauseous while riding on the team bus following a 4-3 loss to the Stars in Dallas. My forehead and palms began to sweat. I had trouble breathing. Matt McConnell, our radio announcer at the time, sat next to me. I asked if we could change seats. I leaned out into the aisle and dropped my head between my knees.

What I didn't know at the time was that I was having my first full-fledged panic attack.

A few nights later, the team hosted a private screening of the movie, *Mighty Ducks 2*, at the Presidential Theater at Disneyland. Lori and I sat in the center of the theater when out of the blue I was struck with the same symptoms. Now granted, I didn't think *MD2* was as good as the original, but it shouldn't have made me ill!

I made an appointment to see the team's physician, Dr. Craig Milhouse. He gave me the once over, and everything checked out. He asked me if I had anything pressing on my mind. I told him that I was feeling a bit homesick and that I missed my dad. He suggested that once the season ended, my dad and I should find a way to spend some time together.

That summer, Lori and I flew back to Chicago. After giving my dad a big bear hug, I informed him that we were going on a road trip and to pack some comfortable clothes.

"Chris," he cautioned, "remember your papa's only got one lung."

"Dad, where I'm taking you, that's all you'll need."

The following morning, Lori and I, along with her mom, Betty, and Lori's sister, Mary Beth, set out to take Dad on a most unforgettable journey.

"Where are you taking me?" Dad kept asking.

"Some place magical."

As we crossed the Illinois-Iowa border, Dad's curiosity piqued. "Iowa? Where are you taking me in Iowa? Are we going gambling?"

"Perhaps later Dad, but not now."

Just past Dubuque, the little hand-painted signs began popping up: *This way to movie site. Dyersville straight ahead.*

Once I turned down the gravel road leading to a ballpark in the middle of a cornfield, Dad turned to me with an impish grin on his face. What better way to reconnect with my dad than to have a game of catch on the Field of Dreams.

Dad was seventy-one years old at the time, but he sprang from the car with the effervescence of a newborn colt, put on his gym shoes, and grabbed a glove. I had purchased some vintage pinstriped jerseys and caps for us to wear. As Mary Beth worked the video camera, she recorded one of the most memorable days of our lives. We played catch, took batting practice, and, of course, took turns walking out of the cornfield. I was pitching to "Shoeless" Ray Madsen, and he was having the time of his life.

Around lunchtime, a passing shower chased us off the field, so we broke for something to eat. By the time we finished eating, we were surrounded by brilliant sunshine. We were faced with a dilemma—should we go riverboat gambling now or go back to the field? It was unanimous—we went back to the field.

No matter how long I live, the memory of my wife with her mom and sister and me with my dad on that baseball diamond in the middle of an Iowa cornfield, will always remain one of the most unforgettable days of my life. Our afternoon was cut short by another sprinkle. But an intersecting double rainbow greeted us when the sun reappeared. It was a perfect ending to a perfect day.

In the guest registry at the Field of Dreams ballpark, my dad wrote, "Memories are the best of life. Thanks Son. Ray Madsen, Chicago, July 21."

Chapter 22

Miracle of Miracles

The summer of 1999 was memorable to me for mixed reasons. I had just signed a new three-year contract to stay on with the Ducks. However, on the day before I signed my contract, my father was diagnosed with a very aggressive form of prostate cancer. As I pressed Dad for more information, he made light of his circumstances, saying to me, "Chris, this is nothing compared to what I went through before." That incredible willpower was what made Dad a sixteen-year lung cancer survivor.

Perhaps, I thought, he could talk himself into beating this cancer, too. But emphysema was beginning to take hold of his remaining lung, and the oncologist concluded that treating the prostate would prove far more beneficial to Dad's well-being than removing it. That meant that this time he would have to undergo radiation and chemotherapy.

Try telling a seventy-six year old that *this* time there would be no choice in the matter.

Dad proceeded begrudgingly with the treatments.

Every time the Ducks schedule would allow me, I'd head back to Chicago and spend some time with my hero. The disgust on my dad's face was plain as day the first time I saw him carting around a miniature oxygen tank. My dad was a very proud man who was always in tune with his appearance. At this stage, there was no getting around his being attached to the flow of oxygen 24-7. And the more his remaining lung was ravaged by the effects of emphysema, the more difficult it became for him to travel any distance at all.

Dad loved to go out to dinner and take in an occasional movie. He also fed off the energy of his grandchildren, Natalie and Nicholas. But perhaps nothing provided him with a more peaceful finish to his day than spending the evening two doors down at the home of his lady friend, Mary Skinner. Each night, Dad would splash on the *Old Spice* and spend time at Mary's. Every now and then, I'd accompany him. I loved the childlike innocence of their kidding one another. Dad was Mary's "stubborn Norwegian." Mary was Dad's "tightfisted Ukrainian."

I also took delight in their nonverbal communication. With Mary's nose in a book, Dad would scour the newspaper. Occasionally, they'd steal a glance at each other, exchange a wink or a smile, and continue reading. Sometimes without uttering a word, they'd speak volumes of love. But most importantly, both were always there for one another. Dad had lost Mom to cancer thirty years ago, and Mary had lost her husband, Glenn, to cancer several years earlier. Mary's caring companionship added a great deal to Dad's life.

In June of 2001, Lori and I returned to Chicago to celebrate my godchild Natalie's elementary school graduation. My brother, Marc, and his wife, Cindy, had the backyard tented as family and friends from across the country came in to attend. As soon as we arrived, I sought out my dad. Through the crowd I spotted him sitting with Mary at his side, holding court with my Uncle Mike, Auntie Dianne, cousin Carrie, Auntie Roe, and her boyfriend Mort. For the first time since his bout with lung cancer eighteen years earlier, Dad looked small to me. His skin, normally tanned, looked ashy. However, when I reached out to hold him, his bear hug was as strong as ever.

I was staying for the next two weeks, but at that moment I didn't want to let go of him. The next fourteen days blew by like the Santa Ana winds—wickedly fast—yet laced with warmth and memories. We went to movies, dinners, shopping trips, rides in the country, and we sat and we talked.

On June 22, it was time for me to return to Orange County. Dad instructed me to wake him for breakfast. At the kitchen table, Dad began what was for me one of the most difficult conversations a father and son are obliged to have.

"Now, you know where my will is?" my dad began.

"I'm pretty sure I do," I replied.

"It's in the briefcase next to my bed along with my safety deposit box key. That's where you'll find the deed to the house."

As he continued, I thought to myself *I told him I'm returning in August. I wonder why he's telling me this now?*

"Now where are you at with your contract?" he asked.

"I have one year left."

"Good. Just continue to do your best."

"I will, Dad."

"Now you'd better get going, or you'll be late for your flight."

As I put the last piece of luggage in the trunk, Dad caught up with me at the front door. With his right hand he cradled the nape of my neck and pulled me close to him.

Touching forehead to forehead he said, "I love you, Son."

"I love you, too, Dad."

We embraced, and as we separated Dad said with tears in his eyes, "You're my little miracle."

With tears in mine I responded, "Dad, if I'm you're little miracle, then you're the greatest miracle a kid could ever ask for."

We embraced once again, and this time I didn't want to let go. As much as I didn't want to admit it, at that moment I sensed *why* my father wanted to have that conversation at breakfast. For an instant, I thought about asking him if he'd like me to stay another day or so. But those last words and the moment seemed so perfect, just as he wanted them to be.

One week to that day, Dad passed away with Mary at his side.

On my return from Dad's services in Chicago, Joshua sent this poem to me by email. He had written it just for me. Every word of every line exemplifies the compassion and empathy of Joshua Souder.

Sorrow times and bad times for all of us to share.

(Joshua reaches out to let me know that I'm not alone and that I have his generous friendship to lean on.)

You are in God's hands, and you have all His love and care.

(Joshua reminds me that the emptiness I'm feeling will one day be filled with God's love and care.)

Heaven is a happy home that your father now shares.

(A happy home was my dad's sincerest wish, and that wish was a reality.)

Living there in happiness, knowing His love and care.

(Joshua's words gave me a vision of my father beaming at being reunited with my mother, his mother and father, his brothers, Sammy and Robert, and Nana and Grandpa Vesio.)

Joshua's thoughtfulness had given me a moment of peace.

Chapter 23

My Sanctuary

loved my dad immensely. The 2001-2002 Mighty Ducks season had a way of reminding me just how much I missed him. There were countless times, whether I was at home or on the road, when I'd pick up the phone to call him only to realize he was gone. Depression, unlike any other I had ever experienced, set in. The most menial tasks, such as picking up after myself, or sifting through the mail, seemed Herculean to me. Lori suggested that I seek out professional help. Being of the same stubborn Norwegian stock I wrote of earlier, I thought I could fight my way through it. Each day was a painful struggle.

Game days, however, became my sanctuary. Once I entered the broadcasting booth, I was able to shelve my inner pain for a few hours. I put on a happy face and called the game that I love free of any mental baggage. The fans, many of whom I had become friends with, were especially supportive following Dad's death. It was so easy to smile when they were around. But once

I'd get in my car and begin the ride home, I'd get off my high and spiral downward.

When the season ended on April 12, 2002, Joshua and his family had taken me up on my earlier offer to watch the game from a luxury suite. How ironic, or was it poetic, that on what would turn out to be my last game as the voice of the Mighty Ducks of Anaheim, the last person I escorted out of the building was Joshua Souder.

And now, three months later while sitting in a darkened den in my brother's home in Chicago, I realized that the booth was gone. The fans were gone. The person I had become was gone. *Would Joshua still see me as his "Broadcasting Booth Buddy?"* I wondered. The shocking news that I would not be back as the voice of the Mighty Ducks left me unable to eat, sleep, and function. Now *I* was the one who was unresponsive, just as Joshua had been years earlier-inside my self-induced emotional coma.

There was a knock on the door. It was my niece, Natalie. "Uncle Chris? I'm finished using my computer if you'd like to use it."

I thanked her, peeled myself off the couch, and walked upstairs. Once I logged on, I noticed an untitled e-mail addressed to me from Joshua. It read:

Dear Chris,
I've decided to rank my all-time favorite broadcasters.
  1. Chris Madsen
  2. Rob Buska, Cal State Fullerton
  3. Steve Physioc, Angels
  4. Sean McCall, Lake Elsinore Storm
  5. Paul Sunderland, Lakers

I also wanted to thank you for believing in me. I honestly don't know what I would do without you. If I didn't have you, tell me what would I do? You inspire me to go on. For as long as I have you to inspire me, I can't go wrong.

From the first time I met you, until that wondrous day [May 3, 1995] *and until now, you have been one of the most inspirational people in my life. You have always encouraged me and believed in me.*

Many times when people see someone like me, they can't see past the disability and see the potential, but you did. And that is really important to me. And because you saw me as a broadcaster, I saw me as a broadcaster. You are my mentor and my role model. And that's given me the confidence to handle the public address announcing duties at my high school basketball game.

Chris, I don't know where your life's journeys will take you, but can you please keep June 12, 2003 available? That's the day of my high school graduation. That also is the day that I plan on getting up out of my wheelchair and walking across the stage to get my diploma. And there's nobody I'd rather have waiting for me on the other side of that stage than you. Please consider being there for me.

> *Your Broadcasting Booth Buddy,*
> *Joshua Souder*
> *Hockey Fan,*
> *Aspiring Broadcaster/Media Relations*
> *[July 22, 2002]*

Opportunities come to those who set out to meet them.

(Further evidence of Joshua's character is revealed in the way he signs his letter, even including his favorite heartfelt belief that opportunities do come to those who set out to meet them.)

Chapter 24

"You're Not Just That . . ."

U pon my return to California, I drove out to the Inland Empire in Riverside County, to visit my special friend. During the forty-five-minute ride along the 91 Freeway, I wondered if there would be a change in the way Joshua would receive me now that I was no longer the voice of his favorite team.

Robyn and John greeted me warmly with handshakes and hugs at the front door. We proceeded to the dining room where we sat, shared a cool drink, and chatted while we waited for Joshua to arrive home from school. Shortly after 3:30, the door-bell rang.

"Joshua's home," Robyn declared.

My heart began to race like Paul Kariya churning down the wing. *When John answers that door, how will Joshua react toward me?* I wondered.

As the door swung open, Joshua shifted his electric

wheelchair into fifth gear and came flying across the room with his patented ear-to-ear grin. As he pulled up along side me, he extended his left arm and we high-fived and hugged just like old times. Then I took a step back. Joshua looked up quizzically and asked, "What?"

"I . . . didn't know how you'd respond."

"What do you mean?"

"Well, for one thing, I'm no longer the voice of the Mighty Ducks."

"So," Joshua shot back with a slight shrug of his shoulders.

"So . . . your 'Broadcasting Booth Buddy' doesn't see himself as the same person anymore."

"The same what?"

"The same person that I was when I was a TV play-by-play announcer."

And with that response, Joshua's innocent grin turned into a full-blown scowl, and his face flushed. He reached out his left hand, caught me by my right forearm, pulled me close, and looked me square in the eye.

"You're not just that! You're more than that! And don't you forget it!"

A chill raced down my spine as I felt the absolute truth of his words. Something inside of me whispered, *"Yes, I am more than that.* I don't need a microphone in my hand or a camera in the room to make a difference in Joshua's life—or anybody else's life, for that matter."

"I care about you for who you are," Josh added, not letting me go, **"not for what you do for a living."**

Joshua's simple affirmation, wrapped around the blunt truth, pulled me back towards reality and out of the emotional haze I was in. It was as if God spoke through him delivering a revelation. In an instant, the source of the pain and distress of my circumstances became crystal clear: I was being tested.

Everyone faces this at some moment in his or her life. I had seen myself solely as the voice of the Mighty Ducks of Anaheim. I couldn't see myself supporting my family as anything but the voice of the Mighty Ducks of Anaheim. I couldn't see myself being of use to others unless I was the voice of the Mighty Ducks of Anaheim. I couldn't see the same reflection in the mirror unless I was the voice of the Mighty Ducks of Anaheim.

I envisioned enjoying the same longevity as Los Angeles broadcasting legends Bob Miller, Chick Hearn and Vin Scully. I saw myself as the voice of the Mighty Ducks for the next 30 years. I had forgotten who *I* really am. Perhaps it was time to rediscover who Chris Madsen really is.

Chris Madsen had always been part of a team. From Pee Wees to Little League, from high school sports and college baseball to work and friendships, I relished in the acceptance of being part of a team. Then, for nine years, I was *literally* a part of a professional hockey team. I was the original soundtrack of the franchise—a dream come true—and what an incredible ride it was.

Now that ride was over. I discovered I had never been captain of my own team; the belief that I could be useful apart from the crew was simply outside my personal realm. But now, because of Joshua, I realized that my purpose in life encompasses much more than just being a member of the squad. It is about the relationships we build in the process. I never would have met Joshua without being part of that terrific team, but now it was time to give *myself* back to me.

This test or revelation all came back to the reason why Joshua and I connected in the first place. I didn't see him as a little boy with Cerebral Palsy confined to a wheelchair. Instead, I viewed Joshua as a beautiful beacon of hope and promise and as a spirit who called out, came in, and enriched my life. I know that my life has been changed forever by our friendship.

Okay, Nicky, I'm ready to answer your question now. You know, the one about what is the best call I ever made. It wasn't just the *best call I ever made;* I think it just might be the greatest call *ever* made.

If I polled sports fans and asked what the greatest call they ever heard was, some might say it was Russ Hodges screaming, "The Giants win the pennant! The Giants win the pennant! The Giants win the pennant!" after Bobby Thompson drilled a home run to win the 1951 National League Championship. Others might argue it was Howard Cosell's rant of "Down goes Frazier! Down goes Frazier!" after George Foreman landed a crushing blow to Joe Frazier to win the World Heavyweight Championship in 1973. Or maybe they'd say it was Al Michaels pondering the question aloud, "Do you believe in miracles? Yessss!" when Team USA upset Russia in the Miracle-on-Ice Game at the 1980 Winter Olympics. Can you think of any others? Bring them on!

Sure, they were all great calls, but the greatest call ever made was on May 3, 1995, when I picked up the phone and called a comatose Joshua Souder. It may have been for an audience of one, but "Joshua shoots! He scores!" is the greatest call I ever made. Period.

Joshua's father prayed for a miracle. His mother was given back her son. Even Joshua himself told me that he's convinced that if I hadn't called that fateful day, he would have died. And if Joshua had died, who would have awakened me and restored the meaning in my life? That's the short list, which is growing every day, because Joshua continues to touch many lives *every day.*

What this call should prove to all of us is that you don't need a microphone in your hand or the power of television behind you to make a difference in another person's life. Sometimes, all it takes is a little genuine faith and a phone call. And it often happens when you least expect it—perhaps even in the middle of a very busy day when you have no time to prepare for it.

Yes, I had an identity crisis. I had seen myself doing worthwhile things *only* while I was a television play-by-play announcer. In my mind, the name Chris Madsen had become worthless without the title of "play-by-play announcer" next to it on a business card.

Joshua was right. I never had been *just* a television play-by-play announcer. I am more than that.

And Joshua, you are not *just* a young "special needs" student in a wheelchair. You *are* more than that. And you're going to prove that to all of us once again when you rise up, through the grace of God, and *walk* across Santiago High School's stage to receive your diploma.

Joshua Souder, you have my solemn promise that on June 12, 2003, I will be waiting for you with open arms on the other side of that stage.

Chapter 25

Joshua Shoots! He Scores! Again!

The evening of June 12, 2003 was marvelously sunny, a fitting backdrop for what promised to be an unforgettable night. Rush-hour traffic left Lori and me inching along the 91 freeway heading east from our home in Orange to Corona.

With my eyes fixed on the taillights directly in front of us, and Bruce Springsteen belting out *The Promise Land* on the CD player, my mind drifted back to the first time Joshua cried out my name at FanFair. I recalled how I knelt down beside him captivated by the lust for life that I witnessed in his big, brown eyes.

I remembered sitting along side him at home games as his left arm pumped in unison with his chant of "Go Ducks go!"

My memory flashed forward to four of the most important words I had ever strung together, "Joshua shoots! He scores!" and the conversation with his father that followed. "We were told several times before that Joshua may not make it through the night, but that was the one time I really feared we were going to lose him." I caught myself shaking my head from side to side, realizing what a terrible loss that would have been for all of us.

I thought of how Joshua reached out to me during two of the most tragic moments of my life, the passing of my dad and the loss of my dream job.

And then there was Joshua's letter where he dubbed me his role model and mentor. At the heart of that letter was an exclusive invitation to be at his side tonight and my promise to be there.

As traffic started to move more freely just before the Route 15 exit to San Diego, my mind clicked off of automatic pilot and was back in the moment. I glanced over at my cell phone and noticed the message light flashing.

Hmmm, I thought to myself, *I don't remember missing a call.*

The call had come from the assignment editor at television station KCBS in Los Angeles. Channel 2 wanted to feature Joshua's promise of walking to receive his diploma on the 11 o'clock news. Without hesitation, I called back and gave the assignment desk operator directions to Santiago High School. As I handed the phone back to Lori, I exclaimed, "This is huge! Josh'll be so excited!"

As we walked up to the football stadium, a line two city blocks long snaked its way through the parking lot. Lori slid in along side Robyn and her family as I was given directions to where I could meet up with Joshua and the rest of the graduates.

I entered a gymnasium that was buzzing with activity. Administrators, teachers, and students in commencement garb scurried to take their proper places as the 2003 graduating class, nearly 800 strong, readied themselves to stroll across campus to greet their adoring families and friends.

"Excuse me? Are you Chris Madsen?" a security guard asked.

"Yes," I nodded.

"Your guests have arrived."

"Please let them in."

Darting across the gym floor were Barb and Terry Notko and their son, Mike. I had asked Terry if he'd man the digital still camera while Mike worked the digital video recorder. Barb thought it would be "neat" to meet Josh.

Under the direction of the event coordinator, John Sawaya, the students filed out of the building in alphabetical order. Once the class reached the football field, a thunderous ovation welcomed them. A crowd of over 8,000 spilled out of the risers along the sidelines and out onto the playing field. In orderly fashion, the students took their assigned seats. Off to the side, Joshua sat by himself, looking handsome in his black graduation cap and gown and silver stole signifying his achievement of graduating with high honors. Draped around his neck were two medallions. Dangling on a teal and black ribbon was Santiago's academic symbol etched in silver. Affixed to a red, white and blue ribbon was a gold medallion from the California Governor's Committee on Employment of People with Disabilities. Josh was one of only six recipients statewide to receive the 19th annual Hal Connelly Scholar-Athlete award that is accompanied by a $1,000 scholarship.

"How're you feeling, Champ?"

"My stomach is churning! I'm so nervous!" Josh said as he extended his left hand and we high-fived each other.

"Hey, every broadcaster gets an adrenaline rush just before he goes on the air. Just take a few deep breaths and drink it all in because tonight's your night, kid!"

For some reason, the image of Mickey talking up Rocky before his rematch with Apollo Creed popped into my mind. As though I had just flicked the switch, a confident ear-to-ear grin beamed across Josh's face.

"Now that's the Joshua Souder that everybody has come

to see! And, besides, I'd be smiling, too, if I were sitting next to as many pretty girls as you are!"

Joshua giggled, and his face flushed.

"I'll see you up on stage, okay?"

"Okay."

"And remember, keep smiling and enjoy yourself!"

"Okay. Hey Chris?"

"Yeah."

"Thanks for being here. It means the world to me."

"Joshua, it means the world to me, too."

The greeting area was decorated with banners, flags, and balloons in the school colors of teal, white and black. A ramp had been erected specifically for Josh off the left side of the stage, and just behind it were folding chairs designated for Terry, Mike, myself and others. Shading my eyes from the sun, I spotted Lori and Barb on the end of Row 11 seated next to Robyn, John and Sarah, as well as Joshua's Grandma Jean, Aunt Jeanette, Aunt Vickie, along with her daughter, Jillian and son, Bryce, and family friends, Bo Lorentzen and Sean McCall. Before I could sit down, a security officer motioned to me.

"There's someone here from Channel 2 to see you."

I hustled down the track.

"Chris?"

"Yes?"

"Hi. I'm Lora McLaughlin, and this is my cameraperson, Suzanne. Have we missed anything?"

"No. They won't be getting to the 'S's' for some time. There are nearly 800 students graduating tonight."

"Eight hundred?"

"That's right. The largest graduating class in the school's history!"

"Can we get Joshua mic'd up real quick?"

"Certainly. Come on, he'd love to meet you."

Sneaking up behind his wheelchair, I whispered in his ear, "Boy, Josh, you're just a magnet for beautiful women tonight. This is Lora McLaughlin from Channel 2."

Josh giggled and extended his left hand to greet her.

"Josh, would you mind if we put a microphone on your graduation gown?" Lora asked.

"Not at all."

As Suzanne hooked up the cable and battery pack, Lora asked Josh, "Do you mind if I interview you right after you receive your diploma?"

"Absolutely."

Lora, Suzanne and I took our seats with the commencement announcers' voices echoing in the background. We exchanged notes on the special friendship Josh and I share. I had my bragging shoes on as I told her that Joshua and his father had been recently hired by radio station KWRM-AM1370 in Corona as studio engineers for California State University in Fullerton and the Rancho Cucamonga Quakes baseball games.

Mike, Terry and Suzanne left their seats to start testing their cameras and sought out the best vantage points to capture the moment. No sooner had I heard the name "Sabat," the first of many beginning with the letter S, Joshua turned on his electric wheelchair and approached his teaching assistant, Nick Williams, at full speed. He nimbly maneuvered his way up the ramp to meet us. As I gazed into the eyes of this incredibly courageous young man, he had the look of a man on a mission. I leaned over and whispered into his ear, "This is the moment you waited your whole life for. When you rise up out of that chair, remember all the time, energy and effort you put into making this happen."

Joshua's eyes remained focused forward. Only his head nodding gave me some indication that I was making contact.

"Now, let's rise up," I said as Mr. Williams grabbed Joshua under his right arm and I under his left. "Stand tall," I whispered as we Velcro-strapped left and right forearms into his walker. "Now, let's give this crowd something to really cheer about!"

On cue, the announcement rang out over the public address system, "With high honors, Joshua Souder."

The commencement proceedings halted as all eyes looked on in amazement as Joshua's left foot inched forward. An audible gasp was heard as the young ladies in the front row responded in unison. As his right foot slid forward, I heard Nick encourage Joshua to "Focus, head up, smile." A young man shouted out, "Go for it Josh!" As his left foot followed, the student body sprung from their seats in a cheer that gave way to pandemonium.

Choked with emotion, I, too, clapped vigorously and cheered Joshua on from the sidelines.

Josh continued.

Right foot.

Then left.

Right foot.

Then left.

By this point, the crowd on both sidelines erupted in a standing ovation and began to pound the aluminum benches with their hands and feet.

Right foot.

Then left.

Slowly the wheels on Joshua's walker churned forward.

The "standing room only" crowd at field level surged forward to a retaining wall in hopes of getting a glimpse of the incredible Joshua Souder.

Right foot.

Then left.

Five more feet to go!

With Mr. Williams guiding the direction of the walker, Joshua Souder reached "the promise land," the podium.

Joshua Souder, the baby that doctors said wouldn't make it through the night. Joshua Souder, the boy the experts once declared should be institutionalized. Joshua Souder, the man with spastic quadriplegic Cerebral Palsy, had just accomplished what was thought to be unthinkable. He walked! He had walked 15 feet in just over a minute.

When Joshua extended his left hand to accept his high school diploma, bedlam erupted. Inside Santiago Football Stadium rose a noise so deafening it would have made any football player envious. Competing against a crowd gone wild, Principal Ruperto Cisneros expressed the thoughts of everyone in attendance when he wrapped his arms around our miracle and declared, "Josh, I am so proud of you!"

Humbled and blushing, Joshua politely said, "Thank you. Thank you."

Then, in workmanlike fashion, seemingly oblivious to the thunderous applause meant solely for him, Joshua handed his leather bound diploma off to Mr. Williams and with the aid of Principal Cisneros, turned his walker around. Set on a course in my direction, the crowd cheered Joshua on.

"We love you Josh!" cried out one graduate.

"Way to go Josh!" chimed another.

Biting down on his lower lip, his right foot dragged along the stage. Grimacing, his left foot followed.

Right foot.

Then left.

His white-knuckled left hand wrapped tightly around the grip of his gait trainer walker.

His right hand wrenched against the silver aluminum

crossbar. Five more grueling steps to go. Then four.

Left foot.

Then right.

Just one more step before Mr. Williams and I wrapped our arms around him.

His left hand could loosen its grip. His shoulders, back and legs would no longer be wretched with pain. Joshua had done it! Only now would he allow himself a smile graced with total satisfaction. Thunderous applause followed Joshua all the while until he settled back into his wheelchair.

All told, Joshua's momentous journey to the podium took about three minutes. Average time for all other graduates: about five seconds.

Sliding his control knob forward, Joshua steered his electric wheelchair back down the ramp where Lora McLaughlin and her cameraperson stood ready and waiting. Mr. Williams and I followed just a few steps behind. Extending her hand-held mic in his direction, Lora asked, "How do you feel Josh? Did you hear that crowd?"

"I feel like I just won the Super Bowl!"

As he pulled away, Lora turned to me and confessed that she thought we were in the middle of an earthquake when the crowd started pounding on their seats.

Terry Notko, positively beaming, put down his camera, grabbed me by the nape of the neck, pulled me close and said, "You've got to feel like you just won the Stanley Cup!"

"Yeah, and Joshua just scored the overtime winner in Game 7!"

"And the beauty of it, Chris, is that Josh wanted *you* here. Not Chris Madsen, the play-by-play announcer, but *you,* the Chris Madsen we *all* love, regardless."

At that moment, it struck me what a gift Joshua had given

me. Of all the people Joshua had touched in his life, he had blessed me with a ring-side seat to witness first hand how an indomitable spirit can overcome just about anything. For nine years I had a rink-side seat to describe the play-making poetry of Paul Kariya, the graceful, goal-scoring touch of "the Great One," Wayne Gretzky, and the magnificent moves of Mario Lemieux—incredibly talented hockey players commonly referred to as "superstars" of their profession.

On June 12, 2003, Joshua Souder redefined what a superstar truly is. God-given talent didn't will Joshua Souder to accomplish this incredible feat. Instead, the *feet* given by God, along with Joshua's incredible talent to will himself, did.

Joshua once told me that when I uttered, "Joshua shoots! He scores!" in his ear on May 3, 1995, "It was like a light bulb went on, and I know that if you hadn't pulled me through, I would have died."

God's plan delivered Joshua, who would make the greatest call I ever *heard*, "You're not just that! You're more than that!" The call registered. I saw the light. He pulled me through, and I chose to live.

"Joshua shoots! He scores!" Four simple words—a lifetime of miraculous gifts.

I've read that miracles have a way of touching the lives of people you don't even know and in places you are not even conscious of. Through a three-minute walk of a lifetime, I witnessed Joshua Souder touch over 8,000 lives. And one of those lives was a wheelchair-bound little boy whose mother stopped Robyn after the commencement ceremony and proclaimed, "Because your son walked tonight, my son believes he'll walk someday too! Thank you so much!"

Not bad for a child doctors once said would just "*be.*" I offer that those same doctors simply forgot to finish the thought, that

Joshua Souder would just "*be*" a precious son, would just "*be*" a loyal friend, would just "*be*" an angel on earth, would just "*be*" an inspiration to many, would just "*be*" a man of unwavering faith, and would just "*be*" a role model for us all.

"Joshua shoots! He scores!" is the greatest call I ever made.

Joshua Souder is the greatest Broadcasting Booth Buddy anybody could ever have.

THE END

EPILOGUE

by Joshua Souder

Why Walk?

It seems as though I had been working on walking at my physical therapy sessions with my physical therapist, Denise Matey, forever. Physical therapy was grueling work, and I hated it. Physical therapy was something that everyone kept telling me I **had** to do. Physical therapy was good for me. Physical therapy would help my posture. Physical therapy would help build up my strength. I hated every step I took. Physical therapy was hard work. Physical therapy was painful. My back ached. My legs hurt. By the time I finished my 30 to 45 minutes of physical therapy, I would be dripping with perspiration. I just hated physical therapy!

Long before I started high school, I knew which one I wanted to go to. I had chosen Santiago because it had a media program that I wanted to be involved in because of my chosen career goals. When I finally started high school, I realized what an exciting yet challenging step it would be towards my goals.

I think I made the decision to walk across the stage to receive my diploma that first day of school my freshman year. I finally found *my* reason to walk.

During my freshman year, I began riding a special adapted bicycle around the track on the football field. Three or four laps a day. Boy, was that work! But, you know what? The other kids would cheer me on as I rode past them or they ran past me. It was so encouraging to me to have my peers cheering me on. Another reason, I thought to myself, for me to walk. Soon, I was using a gait trainer. I had arranged my physical education schedule so that I would be out at the same time that the football team or the basketball team would be doing their workouts. More motivation.

By the time my senior year rolled around, I was so determined that I really felt like pushing myself an extra 10 or 15 steps each time I practiced.

Walking for graduation now had a new meaning. Chris would be at my side, and I knew that my walking for my diploma not only was a goal for me, but it meant something to my mentor.

Then graduation week approached. My instructional assistant, Mr. Williams, and my adaptive PE coach, Val Rodholm, pushed me hard to make sure that I could make the 30 feet from my chair to the principal and back. We took out my walker three or four times a day to practice.

Graduation Night

By the time I arrived at the gym to line up with the other graduates, my nerves were shot, and my stomach was churning. Mr. Williams' words of encouragement just kept echoing in my ear, "Focus, head up, smile." I tried very hard not to be distracted. My goal was in front of me at all times.

I thought of my walking across the stage as a step up towards my college career. And then I thought of a line in Coach Jim LeDuc's poem, "If we ever think to give an excuse, when we reflect on the talents God gave us to use . . ." I couldn't give any excuses now . . . not with Chris and Mr. Williams at my side. Not with my family in the audience. Not with the stadium full of 8,000 people. I was determined, and Chris was by my side. That alone was more than I could ask for.

Your Broadcasting Booth Buddy,

Joshua J. Souder

Joshua J. Souder

AN INVITATION TO SHARE YOUR STORY

TO: You

FROM: Chris Madsen and Joshua Souder

FOR: A new book, titled *"You're Not Just That! You're More Than That!"*

RELEASE DATE: To be determined

WHAT TO BRING: Your true stories of faith, hope, courage, selflessness and generosity

WHEN: Please submit them now

WHERE: Forward your story of 500 words or less to:

JHF Publications, Inc.
1700 East Garry Avenue
Suite 113
Santa Ana, California 92705

PLEASE NOTE:

By submitting your story for consideration, you are granting JHF Publications the exclusive right to edit and use the material in future publications and assigning any copyright of the material to them. The submission must be original and must not have been published elsewhere, and may not infringe upon the rights of others. Complete rules for submission are available upon written request to the address listed above, and must include a self-addressed stamped envelope.

WE LOOK FORWARD TO HEARING FROM YOU!

After receiving his high school diploma, Joshua is assisted by Principal Ruperto Cisneros (left) and teaching assistant, Nick Williams.

Photo by Terry Notko.

Principal Cisneros and Chris Madsen (background) lead the cheering section, as Nick Williams assists Joshua with his gait trainer walker.

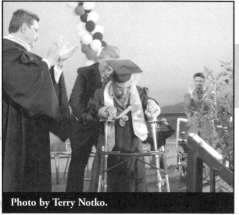

Photo by Terry Notko.

Time for a pep talk prior to Joshua's "Walk of a Lifetime!"

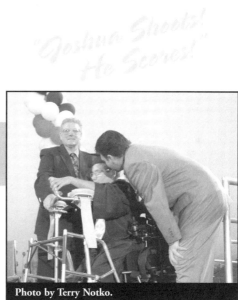

Photo by Terry Notko.

As Nick Williams and Chris look on, Joshua eyes the distance from wheelchair to gait trainer walker.

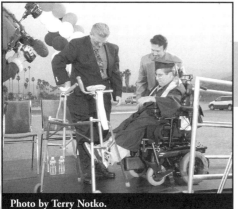

Photo by Terry Notko.

Santiago High School Homecoming Court for 2002: Back Row (l. to r.) Jessica Kirk, Bernard Jackson, Angela Brooks, Ryan Fontanilla, Ryan Smithson, Jonathan Goudy, Anna Pathe. Front Row (l. to r.) Jessica Poore, Joshua, Melanie Espinoza.

Photo from the Souder Family Album.

"Joshua Shoots! He Scores!"

An exhausted Joshua in the summer of 2000 training to walk to receive his high school diploma.

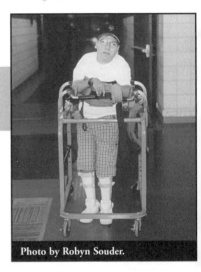

Photo by Robyn Souder.

"Joshua Shoots! He Scores!"

Photo by Chris Madsen.

Nearly twenty years later, Joshua chuckles at the pinstriped jersey Grandma Maryann made for him, while clutching the plush white baseball given to him by Grandma Jean.

"Joshua Shoots! He Scores!"

Joshua's all smiles while surrounded by (l. to r.) Anaheim Angels V.P. of Communications, Tim Mead, Coach Jim LeDuc, and Angels Television Play-by-play Announcer, Steve Physioc.

"Joshua Shoots! He Scores!"

Photo by Robyn Souder.

Chris Madsen, representing the Mighty Ducks in the spring of 2001, at a California elementary school.

Photo © Chris Madsen.

Photo by Lori Madsen.

In what would be Chris' dad's final visit to Southern California in 1999, father and son share a special moment and the view off the Balboa Beach pier.

Three more of Chris' Guardian Angels, (l. to r.) his mother Cecilia, his "Nana" Elizabeth Vesio, and Grandma Marge Kwiatkowski.

Photos by Chris Madsen and the Madsen Family Album.

Photo by Lori Madsen.

A light-hearted moment at the 1996 Mighty Ducks Annual Golf Tournament with (l. to r.) mascot Wild Wing, Chris, Head Coach Ron Wilson, Captain Randy Ladoucer and Radio Announcer, Matt McConnell.

Chris, with sister-in-law Mary Beth Reiniche, following a game at United Center in Chicago.

Photo from the Reiniche Family Album.

Chris, Lori and Ray Madsen memorialize an unforgettable day at the Field of Dreams in Dyersville, Iowa, July 21, 1994.

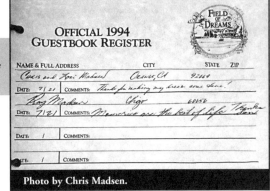

Photo by Chris Madsen.

Chris' dad, Ray Madsen comes out swinging from the world's most famous cornfield.

Photo by Chris Madsen.

The autograph book Chris signed for Joshua during their first-ever meeting at FanFair 1994.

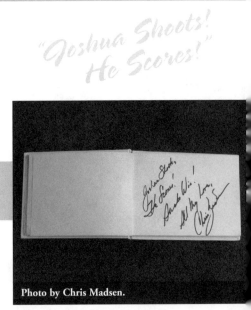

Photo by Chris Madsen.

Chris and Lori Madsen are all smiles following the Mighty Ducks inaugural game, October 8, 1993 against the Detroit Red Wings.

Photo by JD Vercett.

Chris, Lori, their loveable pup Sugar Plum, and Grandma Reiniche celebrate Chris' appointment as the original television voice of the Mighty Ducks at the family's home in Illinois.

Photo by Verne Reiniche.

Chris celebrates Christmas 1991 with (l. to r.) Dad, brother Marc and sister Karen.

Photo by Lori Madsen.

Ten year-old Joshua Souder emerges from the family van with sister Sarah and mom Robyn at an Angels baseball game.

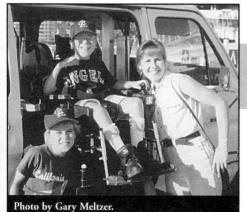

Photo by Gary Meltzer.

Eight year-old Joshua butters-up Mom for more of his favorite dish!

Dear Mom,
Thank you for thinking
bout me. I love the spaghetti
d meatballs you make for me
Love,
Joshua

Photo by Robyn Souder.

Joshua shares a special moment with a wonderful friend, Joni Eareckson Tada.

Photo by Robyn Souder.

Joshua, with microphone in hand, is joined on the set of the 1989 United Cerebral Palsy Star-athon by (l. to r.) Kater Lee, Cal Aylers and the legendary Billy Barty.

Photo from the Souder Family Album.

There's no place like sweet home—Chicago! Six year old Chris with his glove on and ready to "play ball" with brother Marc.

Photo from the Madsen Family Album.

Chris Madsen's "Nana" in 1963 surrounded by her grandchildren (l. to r.) Marc Madsen, Jeff Vesio, Carrie Lynn Vesio, Karen Madsen (forward), Chris and Julie Vesio.

Photo from the Madsen Family Album.

Photo from the Madsen Family Album.

Two year-old Chris seated on his mother's lap for dinner during a Madsen family vacation in Land 'O Lakes, Wisconsin. (l. to r.) Dad, brother Marc and sister Karen.

Joshua and sister Sarah perfecting their belly crawling technique in 1986.

Photo from the Souder Family Album.

Grandma Jean shares a bedtime story in 1986 with her grandchildren (from top to bottom) Jillian Lieuallen, Joshua and Sarah Souder.

Photo from the Souder Family Album.

Five month old Joshua is still smaller than a Cabbage Patch Doll.

Photo from the Souder Family Album.

"Joshua Shoots! He Scores!"

Can you pick out the "real doll" in this picture taken in 1985? It's Joshua, of course!

"Joshua Shoots! He Scores!"

Photo by Robyn Souder.

John's hand on his son's belly gives you some scale as to just how tiny Joshua was at two weeks old.

"Joshua Shoots! He Scores!"

Photo by Robyn Souder.

Joshua John Souder, born July 4, 1984 at the Portland Maine Medical Center Neonatal Intensive Care Unit.

"Joshua Shoots! He Scores!"

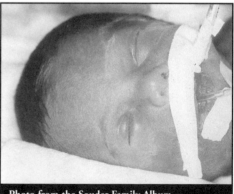

Photo from the Souder Family Album.

"Joshua Shoots! He Scores!"
The Greatest Call I Ever Made

Chapter by chapter photo credits

Chapter 1- Nicky Madsen by Chris Madsen

Chapter 2- Chris Madsen and Joshua Souder at Mighty Ducks FanFair 1994 by
   Robyn Souder

Chapter 3- Top Row L to R: Auntie Roe, Karen Madsen, Marc Madsen, Raymond Madsen
   Bottom Row L to R: Chris Madsen, Cecilia Madsen 1970 © Chris Madsen

Chapter 4- Christmas 1967 © Chris Madsen

Chapter 5- Chris Madsen at Lewis University entrance by Ed Vucinic

Chapter 6- Chris Madsen, Lewis University baseball by Mike Corbett

Chapter 7- L to R: Chris Madsen and JD Vercett by Lori Madsen

Chapter 8- Lori and Chris Madsen © Chris Madsen

Chapter 9- 1993 Audition Video by Chris Madsen

Chapter 10- Audition Video Box Cover by Chris Madsen

Chapter 11- Arrowhead Pond of Anaheim by John Siedlinski

Chapter 12- State of California/State of Florida by D.M. Steele Company

Chapter 13- Cecilia Madsen © Chris Madsen

Chapter 14- Chris Madsen auctioneer by Jim Duran

Chapter 15- Joshua Souder in the isolette 1984 by Robyn and John Souder

Chapter 16- Joshua Souder behind the steering wheel of a fire truck by Robyn Souder

Chapter 17- Top Row L to R: Chris Madsen, Robyn Souder
   Bottom Row L to R: Lori Madsen, Joshua Millsap, Joshua Souder,
   Pam Williams © Chris Madsen

Chapter 18- Joshua Souder by Robyn Souder

Chapter 19- Joshua Souder in the Mighty Ducks locker room at FanFair 1994 by
   Robyn Souder

Chapter 20- Joshua Souder at Challenger Baseball © Robyn Souder

Chapter 21- L to R: Raymond Madsen and Chris Madsen at Field of Dreams by
   Lori Madsen

Chapter 22- L to R: Mary Skinner and Raymond Madsen by John Siedlinski

Chapter 23- L to R: Chris Madsen, Joshua Souder and Sarah Souder at the Arrowhead
   Pond of Anaheim, April 12, 2002 by Robyn Souder

Chapter 24- L to R: Chris Madsen and Joshua Souder by Robyn Souder

Chapter 25- L to R: Suzanne-Camera Operator, Lora McLaughlin and Joshua Souder by
   Terry Notko

For more inspiring photos of Joshua Souder visit the GALLERY at www.joshuashoots.com.

PUBLICATIONS

www.jhfpublications.com

www.joshuashoots.com